MW00817499

APACHERIA

True Stories of Apache Culture 1860–1920

W. MICHAEL FARMER

TWODOT®

GUILFORD, CONNECTICUT
HELENA, MONTANA

A · TWODOT® · BOOK

An imprint of Globe Pequot
A registered trademark of Rowman & Littlefield

Distributed by NATIONAL BOOK NETWORK

Copyright © 2017 W. Michael Farmer

All rights reserved. No part of this book may be reproduced in any form or by any electronic or mechanical means, including information storage and retrieval systems, without written permission from the publisher, except by a reviewer who may quote passages in a review.

British Library Cataloguing in Publication Information available

Library of Congress Cataloging-in-Publication Data

Names: Farmer, W. Michael, author.
Title: Apacheria : true stories of Apache life, 1860–1920 / W. Michael
    Farmer.
Description: Guilford, Connecticut : TwoDot, 2017. | Includes bibliographical
    references and index.
Identifiers: LCCN 2017046578 (print) | LCCN 2017047245 (ebook) | ISBN
    9781493032808 (e-book) | ISBN 9781493032792 (pbk. : alk. paper)
Subjects: LCSH: Apache Indians—History—Juvenile literature. | Apache
    Indians—Social life and customs—Juvenile literature.
Classification: LCC E99.A6 (ebook) | LCC E99.A6 F37 2017 (print) | DDC
    979.004/9725—dc23
LC record available at https://lccn.loc.gov/2017046578

∞™ The paper used in this publication meets the minimum requirements of American National Standard for Information Sciences—Permanence of Paper for Printed Library Materials, ANSI/NISO Z39.48-1992.

Printed in the United States of America

For Corky, my best friend and wife

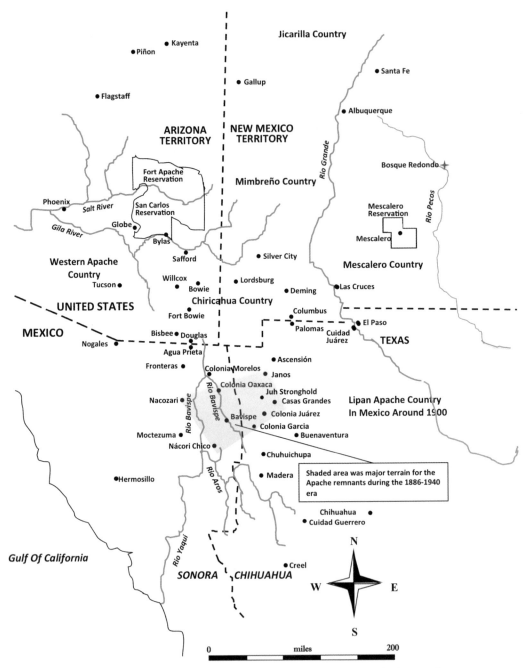

The Apacheria Prior to 1886. (Towns built after 1886 are shown for points of reference.)
MICHAEL FARMER

CONTENTS

Map of the Apacheria Prior to 1886. iv
Acknowledgments viii
Preface ix

Introduction xi
    Apache Culture xi
    Apache Bands and Lifeways. xii
    Apache Religious Belief xvi
    Apache Courtship and Family Life xviii
    Apache Training and Codes of Honor .xxii

Part 1. Apache Raiding and Warfare. 1
    Apache Warrior Women. 3
    1861 Apache Diplomacy on the El Paso Road 5
    "My Father Was a Good Man; He Killed Lots of White Eyes". 7
    Juh's Assassination of Lt. Howard Cushing 10
    Victorio 13
    A Victorio Cavalry Ambush. 17
    Nana, Victorio's Segundo 20
    Geronimo and the Arroyo Fight 23
    Sierra Madre Apaches. 27

Part 2. The Geronimo Wars 30
    Geronimo's Only Capture 31
    Geronimo's First Breakout from San Carlos, 1878 34
    Geronimo's Second Breakout from San Carlos, 1881 37
    Geronimo's Third and Last Breakout from San Carlos, 1885 41
    Geronimo's Final Surrender and the Law of Unintended Consequences 45

Part 3. Apache Scouts 49
   Apache Scouts: Heroes, Outlaws, and Survivors 50
   Al Sieber, Chief of Scouts 54
   Apache Scout Power. 56
   Apache Scouts and the Salt River Cave Fight. 58
   Apache Scout Tzoe, "Peaches". 60
   Chato: Survivor and Apache Judas? 63

Part 4. The Apache Kid: Trials, Escape, Renegade 66
   Trials of the Apache Kid. 67
   The Escape of the Apache Kid 70
   Apache Kid, Renegade. 73

Part 5. Massai—The Warrior Who Escaped. 77
   Massai's Early Life. 78
   Massai and Gray Lizard Escape from the Florida Train for Prisoners of War . . 81
   Massai Takes A New Wife 85
   Massai Goes to the Happy Place 88

Part 6. Apache Prisoners of War. 91
   Apache Prisoners of War for Twenty-Seven Years. 93
   Apache Prisoners of War at Mount Vernon Barracks 96
   Mescaleros Sent to Florida with the Chiricahuas Get an Early Release 100
   Apache Prisoners of War Sent to Fort Sill 103
   Apache Prisoner of War Years at Fort Sill. 107
   Geronimo Asks President Theodore Roosevelt to Let His People Go 111
   Geronimo's Twenty-Three Years in Captivity 114

Part 7. Early Life on the Mescalero Reservation 117
   The Mescaleros Penned Up at Bosque Redondo 119
   Five Hundred Mescaleros Disappear Overnight from Bosque Redondo 122
   Victorio on the Mescalero Reservation 125
   Invasion of the Mescalero Reservation 129
   Agent W. H. H. Llewellyn, Tata Crooked Nose. 131
   The Jicarilla Come to Mescalero. 134
   Agent V. E. Stottler, Tata Loco 138
   "Kill the Indian . . . Save the Man". 141

Part 8. The Chiefs of the Mescaleros 143
   Cadette 144
   Natzili, Sombrero, and Solon Sombrero .148
   Magoosh, Chief of the Lipan Apache 151
   San Juan 154
   Peso, Last Mescalero Chief 157
   Chiricahua Prisoners of War Return to Mescalero, New Mexico 160
   Naiche, Last Chief of the Chiricahua Apaches 163
   The Parallel Lives of Mangas, Son of Mangas Coloradas, and Naiche,
     Son of Cochise 167
   Asa Daklugie: "It Took Four Years to Get Him to Talk" 170
   The Last White Eye 173

Epilogue 176
Endnotes 179
Additional Reading and Information Resources 183
Index 184
About the Author 191

Acknowledgments

There have been many contributors to this effort. A few deserve special mention. Erin Turner, editor at Two Dot, chose to make this book possible and has been very supportive and helpful throughout its development.

Melissa Star helped edit the text, providing an additional pair of eyes for finding errors and inconsistencies, and has been a major contributor to the quality of the work.

Lynda Sánchez shared rare photographs from her collection developed over years of research with Eve Ball and helped keep me grounded in the historical realities of the Apache People.

Ms. Teddie Moreno, Library Specialist for Archives and Special Collections, has provided great support in providing me photographs I requested from the New Mexico State University Rio Grande Collection of photographs. Ms. Coi E. Drummond-Gehrig, Digital Image Collection Administrator for the Denver Public Library, was very helpful in acquiring the image for Lieutenant Stottler and the Jicarilla family. Tom Schmidt, Reference Desk Coordinator for the Sharlot Hall Museum Library and Archives in Prescott, Arizona, helped provide a hard-to-find image of the Apache Kid and other prisoners at the 1889 Globe Trial.

I would be remiss not to express to the many readers of the original drafts of these essays my sincere appreciation for their support and comments.

Finally, to my wife, Carolyn, I owe much for her encouragement and support without which this work would not have been possible, and it is to her that this book is dedicated.

Preface

THE HISTORY OF THE APACHES IN THE LAST HALF OF THE NINETEENTH CENTURY AND the early years of the twentieth century is filled with stories of strength, cunning, courage, and tragedy. The Apaches, if equally armed, were often far better warriors in the land of their fathers than their white counterparts, who faced tough, implacable enemies in a great, unknown wilderness. However, what the Anglos lacked in knowledge of the land and fighting skills, they more than made up for with nerves of steel, unending numbers, virtu-ally unlimited supplies, and a belief that their social mores and Christian religious beliefs were clearly superior to those of the Apaches. The Anglos' courage, numbers, and supplies forced the Apaches on to small bits of land called reservations, which by treaty were to be protected with the same rights as "foreign countries" within the United States. The Anglos didn't keep their agreements, took back much of the reservation land, and even attempted to change Apache lifeways to more nearly match those of Anglo society. As a result, the battle moved from a fight for land to one for souls, and it continues to this day.

This book draws on the work of respected historians and ethnologists and visual imag-ery from the times to provide the general reader a collection of true stories with associated visual images of the life and times of the Apaches from about 1860 to 1920, a period of brutal wars with Mexicans and Anglos, internment on reservations (some often virtual prisoner of war camps), and government-directed attacks on their lifeways. My intent with these stories is to give the reader a three-dimensional historical perspective that is possi-ble only by telling of events, times, and persons seen through a white eye and through an Apache eye to eliminate the historical parallax that develops when only one point of view is given. These stories show the Apaches were no more savage than the Mexicans or Anglos, who ultimately forced them to surrender their wild and free ways, and the stories help to focus additional light on an epic saga in American history far too long in the shadows. The Apaches, taught to endure hardship and suffering from the time they were off their cradle-boards, and to make war with no quarter given or expected in a hard, unforgiving land, have survived the years of hardships imposed by an often ignorant and uncaring government and made their way to stand tall and proud as survivors who leapt from the Stone Age to the Atomic Age in a generation. The facts of the stories salute their courage and strength.

Only a few of the stories that fill this great, uniquely American saga can be presented here. While these stories are by necessity brief, the interested reader can find additional information and details in the notes and additional reading list of trusted historical and cultural work that follow.

W. Michael Farmer
Smithfield, Virginia
September 2017

Introduction

Geronimo's surrender to the U.S. Army on September 4, 1886, brought to an end more than 25 years of sustained conflict between the Apaches and Americans and 250 years of conflict with Spaniards and Mexicans. For forty years after the surrender of Geronimo, most Anglos and Mexicans knew little or nothing about the actual lifeways of the Apaches or their wars. Information for the histories that were written during that time came, for the most part, from military records, reservation agent reports, and newspapers. And Apaches were almost invariably portrayed in popular accounts as howling demons murdering, scalping, raping, torturing, and burning anyone or anything that stood in their way. They were consummate villains, and the public was fascinated.

Nearly twenty years after he surrendered, Geronimo, the best-known Apache "villain," rode his horse (along with five other well-known chiefs from the Indian wars) in Theodore Roosevelt's 1905 inaugural parade. Next to the president, he was the second-most popular man in the parade. In the years since his surrender, he had become a celebrity, appearing in parades and expositions all over the United States as an Apache "patriot." As he rode down Pennsylvania Avenue, men threw their hats in the air and yelled, "Hooray for Geronimo!" He was, in the disgusted words of Woodworth Clum, son of the famous San Carlos Indian agent John Clum, who was the only man actually to capture Geronimo, "Public Hero Number Two."

Since Roosevelt's inaugural parade, popular books and movies have done little, with a few notable exceptions, to change the ideas that Apaches were just look-alike, think-alike savages living in brush huts in the deserts of Arizona and New Mexico. Seeing for the first time, from the Apache point of view, the Apache wars, the Apache transition to the reservations, and bumbling government attempts to change Apaches to second-class Anglos is an enlightening experience as Eve Ball, the great chronicler of Apache oral history, and other reliable historians and ethnologists who carefully studied the Apaches discovered.

Apache Culture

Understanding Apache history requires understanding the basics of their culture, which includes their origins, their bands, their lifeways, their courting customs, their family relationships, their raising of children, and their codes of honor. Apache culture in all its variants sustained its people, enabling them to endure and survive in a hard, unforgiving land, to repel attacks on the beliefs and lifeways of their grandfathers, and to hold at bay and—in some cases—to drive away enemies that vastly outnumbered them and had much greater resources in material.

APACHE BANDS AND LIFEWAYS

The term "Apache" encompasses a number of distinct groups or so-called "bands" with many differences and similarities depending on location. How many bands there were and how many subdivisions were within those bands is debated among anthropologists. The Apacheria roughly covered western Texas, New Mexico, Arizona, and the northern Mexico states of Chihuahua and Sonora, and late in the eighteenth century, Spaniards gave Apache bands who lived in those areas names we still use today. To the east of the Rio Grande lived the Mescaleros, the Jicarillas, and the Lipans. These bands were basically plains Indians driven west across the Pecos River and into the western mountains by the Comanches, who dominated and controlled the southern plains with their horsemanship, rifles they got from French traders in the north, and no-quarter-given brutality. While the Apaches and Comanches were blood enemies, they often worked together to drive out the *Indah* (white people), but as late as 1869 Comanches were still raiding Apache rancherías (camps) in central New Mexico.

Apache Scouts Trailing, by Herman W. Hansen, ca. 1890–1900, illustrates the popular concept of Apaches being fierce unrelenting trackers and warriors.

The Mescaleros lived in the Sacramento Mountains in central New Mexico with the great mountain Sierra Blanca anchoring the northern end of their range and the Río Pecos roughly defining the eastern edge of the plains over which they roamed. There were also significant bands of Mescaleros in the Guadalupe Mountains on the Texas–New Mexico border, the Davis Mountains, a hundred miles farther south near the Big Bend country, and west into the Mexican State of Chihuahua.

The Jicarilla Apache lived in the mountains of northern New Mexico but hunted buffalo on the plains to the east often beyond the Río Pecos, and the Lipans lived on the Texas plains, at times trading with the Comanches and their Kiowa allies until smallpox forced them to break into smaller bands to avoid contagion of the entire band. Some of these bands crossed the Río Grande into Chihuahua, and some even went to the eastern edges of the Sierra Madre, which the Apaches called the Blue Mountains.

On the west side of the Río Grande in New Mexico and toward the south were the Western Apaches and the Chiricahua Apaches. The Western Apache bands and associated groups included White Mountain, Cibecue, San Carlos, Southern Tonto, and Northern Tonto bands whose lands began in eastern Arizona and stretched west.[1]

The Chiricahuas are usually divided into the eastern, central, and southern bands. The Eastern Chiricahua, or Chihenne (Red Clay People for the red clay stripe they often wore on their faces), occupied the territory between what is now the Arizona–New Mexico border and the Río Grande. The Central Chiricahuas, also known as Chokonens, occupied the Chiricahua and Dragoon Mountains of southeastern Arizona. The Southern Chiricahuas, or Nednhis, ranged across northern Sonora and Chihuahua and had strongholds in the northern Sierra Madre. In the 1837–1862 era, there was a fourth, smaller band of Chiricahuas, the Bedonkohes, also known as Mimbreños, Warm Springs, or Ojo Caliente Apaches, who ranged western New Mexico in the Mimbres Mountains, which is often referred to as the Black Range. Mangas Coloradas was the Mimbreños' greatest chief, who first united and led his people around 1837. After his murder in 1863, the Bedonkohes were gradually absorbed into the other three Chiricahua bands. His successor, Victorio, also a mighty chief, led the Mimbreños until he was wiped out at Tres Castillos in Chihuahua in October 1880. The Chiricahuas were famous for such warrior legends as Cochise (Chokonen), Juh (Nednhi), and Geronimo (Bedonkohe), a *di-yen* (medicine man) for Cochise's second son, Naiche, who at nineteen became chief of the Chokonen Chiricahua after his brother, Taza, who had been trained for leadership and appointed chief by Cochise, unexpectedly died.

The common denominators for all the bands were that they spoke some dialect of Athabascan and had similar lifeways in terms of acceptable foods, avoidance customs, and views toward marriage. The Mimbreños and Chiricahuas were closer in culture to the Mescaleros than any other bands. Some physical differences between the bands are easy to see. Like plains Indians, the eastern Apaches lived in tipis, wore low-cut moccasins, and often wore blankets draped around them like Roman togas. Western Apaches mostly lived in brush shelters called wickiups and wore boot-like moccasins that had a leather button the size of half a dollar on the toe and shafts that could be pulled up above their knees. These people rarely wore blankets.

All the Apache bands had Athabascan (or as some linguists now prefer, Dene) as their common language. Athabascan, a beautiful, complex, tonal language, is hard to learn and hard to speak and write because of all the tonal signs and accents needed to capture correct pronunciation. There are three major Athabascan dialects and many subvariants spoken by three First Nations groups: Apache, Navajo, and Chippewa (Alaskan and northern Canadian tribes). Anthropologists and archeologists have traced the migration of Athabascan-speaking people south along the eastern edge of the Rockies from the valleys of the Mackenzie and Yukon Rivers in the Pacific Northwest, starting about AD 1000. Between AD 1300 and AD 1500, the people we call Apache had probably pushed well into the Southwest and lived in the area the historians call the Apachería.

Although the dialects between the three groups are different, Apaches in the various bands could understand one another's speech and that of the Navajos, who were their blood enemies in the mid-nineteenth century. (Anthropologists debate whether the Navajos split off from the initial migration south or if they were a secondary group that followed a little later.)[2]

The Apache had restrictive diets, the specifics of which often depended on the band. For example, no Apache ate bears or coyotes or would kill them except in self-defense because they were sacred animals; some wouldn't eat jackrabbits, but cottontails were all right; some wouldn't eat snakes or things that ate snakes, such as road runners; some wouldn't eat fish or pork; and none ate creepy-crawly things like insects or centipedes. Contrary to reservation agent reports in the late nineteenth century, the pre-reservation Apaches were personally very clean, bathing every day, even when the creeks iced over. Their personal hygiene was never in question until they were forced into squalor on the reservations, where water resources and privacy were often very limited.

The Apaches had to develop phenomenal memories to survive. They didn't have a written language and so, through stories repeated often by their fathers, uncles, and grandfathers at firesides, they handed down with great accuracy family histories and stories through the generations. Messages in war and peace between chiefs and leaders had to be accurately remembered, and the shapes of mountains in the distance and every twist and turn on a trail had to be remembered to navigate across a seemingly endless country that had no markers except what nature provided.

The Lookout, by Herman w. Hansen, ca. 1900, illustrates the basic vigilance Apaches had to maintain to survive raiding Anglos, Mexicans, Navajos, and Comanches.

APACHE RELIGIOUS BELIEF

Mid-nineteenth-century Apaches were a dry-land warrior people who believed in one creator god, *Ussen*. They also had strong beliefs in and fear of ghosts and witches, which is why upon a person's death, all their belongings, including their lodges, were destroyed by fire, the fear being that the ghost might want something they had left behind and come back for it, giving the survivors ghost sickness. (Some anthropologists have pointed out that burning the possessions of the deceased also prevents interfamily fighting over inheritances.)

The Apaches believed that *Ussen* sent to earth White Painted Woman, who had two sons, Child of the Water and Killer of Enemies, who killed the giants terrorizing the earth. They believed *Ussen* also gave special supernatural power to individuals, who were

1898 colorized photo by F. A. Rinehart, courtesy of National Archives, shows Geronimo (Goyahkla), who was once accused and sometimes thought of as being a witch, even to his own children.
PHOTO COURTESY OF LIBRARY OF CONGRESS

to use their power to help the People. These powers ranged from healing ceremonies for particular ailments to sensing the direction from which enemies came to identifying witches and their powers.

The Apache understanding of witches differed from the beliefs the Europeans brought to America. The Apaches believed that anyone might be given a particular supernatural power to cure a particular ailment or provide support in many of their lifeways. The Apache believed that the gifts of power were intended to be used for the good of the People, but that the powers themselves were neither good nor bad. The person holding the power was called a *di-yen* (medicine man or woman), and a *di-yen* who used their gifts for evil purposes was a witch. Apaches said a person suffering from a witch's evil was "witched."

One of the most famous Apache *di-yens* was *Goyahkla*, One Who Yawns, or as he was known by his Mexican name, Geronimo. The historical record shows that Geronimo had Power to see the future or events taking place far away, that he had healing ceremonies he carried out for his People, and that, at least once, he was accused of being a witch.

A witched person might be saved from an evil influence through the services of a *di-yen* who had a unique ceremony to overcome a particular kind of ailment. However, a *di-yen*, after examining the victim, might decide the victim was too far gone, or that the evil Power was greater than their own, and refuse to help the victim. If a *di-yen* did agree to help a witched person, their ceremonies might, for example, cover separate sings over four nights, or one all-night sing involving the use of special icons or medicines that were helped and guided by the *di-yen's* Power.

In some ceremonies, the *di-yen* might appear to literally suck the evil out of a person. Those watching the ceremony would see the *di-yen* produce a two- or three-inch sliver of human bone from the victim shaped like an arrow with the head and nock red and the middle blue and wrapped with strands of human hair. In other cases, the *di-yen* might locate the evil source as something hidden within the living area of the victim, perhaps a six-inch shaft covered with beaded leather, feathers, and strands of human hair. In all cases, these witch weapons were burned, and in burning, they made loud, explosive pops that sounded like guns going off when the evil was destroyed.

The Mescalero Apaches, in particular, were highly sensitive to beliefs in witches and witchcraft. In the days before the reservations, witches were destroyed by their being tied upside down on wheels, their heads just above a fire of hot coals. When reservation conditions were especially hard at the beginning of the twentieth century, instances of perceived witchcraft grew. Anything out of the ordinary a person did might put them under immediate suspicion of being a witch. For example, a man seen standing in the middle of the road waving a bandanna at sunrise, or, someone spontaneously rehearsing dance steps or ceremonial songs outside normal practice times might fall under suspicion of witchcraft. Regardless of an Apache's band, a proof positive measure of a person being a witch was a knowing involvement in incest or any other sexual perversion. On the reservations, accused witches were hung by their wrists, their feet just off the ground, until they admitted their evil, and then they were burned.

APACHE COURTSHIP AND FAMILY LIFE

Among all the tribes in the Southwest, Apache women were the most chaste. John Cremony in his *Life Among the Apaches* relates that during the two years he was part of the army command overseeing Bosque Redondo, when hundreds of Apache women mingled freely with the bluecoats, not a single case occurred where an Apache woman "surrendered her person to any man outside of her tribe."

A 1903 Edward S. Curtis photograph of Sigesh, an Apache maiden, proud and beautiful, who would command a high bride gift
COURTESY OF LIBRARY OF CONGRESS

Although Apache women were very chaste, they were also as flirtatious as women from other tribes, who were much freer with their favors, and, therefore, Apache women were highly sought after. A girl was assumed ready for marriage as soon as she reached her maturity and had her *Haheh* (Puberty Ceremony). In the days before the reservations, she had her *Haheh* as soon as she reached her menarche, even if the band was on the move or being chased. At the end of her *Haheh*, the now marriageable young woman might be chased in a race with the young men wanting to court her until the one she wanted (sometimes didn't want) caught her, and, if she agreed to accept her suitor and her mother was approached with an expensive bride gift, she was married in a matter of days. This meant that in the early pre-reservation days some girls were married as early as their twelfth or thirteenth birthdays, although marriage that early was generally rare. On the reservation, agents decided the Indians only needed to have one *Haheh* a year and that it could serve for all the girls who had reached maturity in that year. For the Mescaleros, the directive was for the *Haheh* to be held in early July (usually around the fourth).

Men were assumed ready for marriage after they proved themselves warriors and potential providers. To be a warrior, a boy had to go on four raids and acceptably serve as an acolyte, doing camp chores and helping the warriors, while staying out of the way of danger. If they did well, then the warriors accepted them as men, and by the time they had been on a few raids as warriors up front where the danger was, they had enough respect, property, and power to ask a family who had an eligible daughter for a wife, and if accepted, to live with his wife near her mother.

As a warrior, the man had to take enough plunder during raids that he could give his future in-laws a "gift" if he wanted a bride. During courtship, the couple often went through many "accidental" meetings at water sources or along trails when there were several others nearby, and they danced together at tribal dances where the women got to pick their dance partners.

When the warrior felt reasonably confident the woman he wanted would accept him, he tied his pony in front of the lodge of his intended. If she fed and watered the pony and brought it back to the warrior's lodge within three days, then she showed that she had accepted his proposal. Often, she made the pony wait a day or two without water or feed to demonstrate that she wasn't overly eager for the union and that an expensive gift for her mother was expected.

Once the woman returned the pony, the man sent his representative to his future mother-in-law to negotiate the bride gift (usually, for Mescaleros this was two to four horses plus less valuable items such as tipi canvas or cooking pots). Once the bride's mother accepted the potential husband, there was a flurry of activity while a new lodge was prepared near her mother's lodge and the bride was instructed by the women of the band in the ways of good husbandry. The future groom often found a place for the couple to camp alone for a week or two after they began living together. Unmarried men and women were usually so shy around each other they might not even discuss sex before they were married. Marriage ceremonies, if held at all, were small affairs often followed by a feast and dancing with the couple slipping away. It was not unusual for the couple to just show up at their lodge on the appointed day and begin life together.

The lodge was assumed to be the woman's, and while she was subservient to her husband, she was much more a partner than a slave. If troubled matrimonial times came, she went back to her mother and stayed, and might, after a while, declare they were divorced. If a man wanted to divorce his wife, he said so and left. (All this was rare in days before the reservations but got to be a problem on the reservations by the turn of the last century.)

Polygamy by Mescalero men and those of other bands was rare but not unusual. If a man could afford a second or third wife, it was his choice to make, and it was fully acceptable if he chose to have more than one wife. For Mescaleros, the second or third wife was almost always the sister of the first wife. Avoidance customs, such as the husband not seeing his mother-in-law, made it difficult to impossible to function with more than one mother-in-law in the same band, and if the women were not sisters, they would want their own lodges, which increased the cost of the second wife. The old Apaches were wise people.

Chiricahua and Jicarilla Families

Chiricahua

Jicarilla

Naiche (Second Son of Cochise) and His Wife Ha-o-zinne, 1884

Runner Ed Ladd and Family, 1886

Comparison of Chiricahua and Jicarilla families near the end of the nineteenth century. 1884 photograph of Chiricahua family Naiche and Ha-o-zinne; 1886 photo of Jicarilla family of Runner Ed Ladd. PHOTO OF NAICHE AND HA-O-ZINNE, COURTESY OF NATIONAL ARCHIVES. PHOTO OF JICARILLA FAMILY OF RUNNER ED LADD COURTESY OF DENVER PUBLIC LIBRARY, WESTERN HISTORY COLLECTION X-32943.

The Apaches had strict avoidance rules. For example, an Apache man must avoid ever seeing or being seen by his mother-in-law or female cousins after their maturity, and conversely, women had to avoid seeing male cousins.

Marital infidelity was extremely rare. There was no penalty if an Apache man was unfaithful to his wife, but she was free to toss him out of her lodge and return to her parents. If a wife was found unfaithful to her husband, he could beat her, cut off the end of her nose to make her ugly and unattractive to other men, divorce her, or kill her, and he was expected to go for the blood of the man who was her paramour.

Apaches rarely raped or otherwise abused women they took in raids. These women, originally taken as property to be used and maintained, might become slaves or wives bearing children if they were strong enough to survive camp life. Their treatment was often good enough that there are anecdotal stories and historical records of Mexican women taken by Apaches who refused to return to their families after a ransom for them was offered.

To gain some idea of the differences in how eastern and western Apaches dressed, compare the photographs of Chiricahua and Jicarilla families taken near the same time (1884 and 1886). The Chiricahua family on the left is Naiche and his youngest wife, Ha-o-zinne. He had three wives: Nah-de-yole (the oldest), E-clah-heh, and Ha-o-zinne, the third and youngest. None of these women were from the same family. Ha-o-zinne returned to Mescalero, New Mexico, with Naiche (Nah-de-yole and E-clah-heh died and were buried at Fort Sill) after they were released as prisoners of war from Fort Sill, Oklahoma. She died of a heart attack while on a walk near her home on the Mescalero Reservation in 1913, soon after her release from captivity.

The picture of Naiche and Ha-o-zinne shows that Naiche wears classic western Apache high-shaft moccasins with a leather button about the size of half a dollar at their toe. Neither he nor Ha-o-zinne use blankets; their clothes are close fitting and their hair is long and straight. The picture was taken about a year after General Crook and his scouts returned runaway Apaches from their camps in the Sierra Madre in 1883. Naiche and Ha-o-zinne are said to have had a baby boy stolen from them by a nurse in 1888.

The photograph of the Jicarilla family shows Runner Ed Ladd, his wife, and two children. Note the adults and oldest child are wearing blankets. Their moccasins are the low-cut plains type (although this is hard to see in the photo). The adults wear their hair in braids, unlike the long, straight hair worn by Naiche and Ha-o-zinne. By 1896, Mescalero Agent V. E. Stottler forced Mescalero men to cut their hair short and to dress like white men. In their opinion they no longer looked like Mescalero men and were therefore no longer attractive to Mescalero women, and that was a primary reason why they didn't want to change their hair or their clothes.

APACHE TRAINING AND CODES OF HONOR

Boys and girls, from the time they were off their cradleboards (*tsachs*), trained with toy bows and reed arrows, and later with real weapons, to be deadly accurate. They used their arrows to shoot at anything any time. They were taught to use slings and had mock battles where a stone might be slung hard enough to break an arm or leg, and it was incumbent on the participants to learn to dodge, hide, and retaliate or suffer the consequences. Apache men underwent demanding physical training beginning in their early years. Training included running for miles in searing desert heat with enough discipline to hold water in their mouths without swallowing it, which forced them to breathe through their noses. Apache men were so physically fit that they had enough stamina often to outrun horses over long distances of fifty to one hundred miles.

Apaches rarely took scalps unless one was required for a ceremony or in revenge. The Apaches had an aversion to handling things of or from the dead because of their powerful beliefs in ghosts. On most war raids, mutilation of enemy corpses was also rare, but when there was time away from being chased, Apaches were masters of torture for the living. They might bury enemies up to their chests in sand, slice off their eyelids, and make them stare at a blazing sun, while their exposed bodies were covered with cooked mescal to bring armies of ants; they might tie an enemy in the sun for days next to water just out of reach, or tie them upside down like they were witches to roast their heads over the coals of a hot fire but kept just far enough away that they might live for days; or an enemy might be dragged through cactus, or have the soles of their feet cut in thin ribbons and made to run across the desert.

Codes of honor also dictated how Apaches lived. The details of their systems of honor varied from band to band, and not every person within a band lived exactly by a generally accepted code. Nevertheless, history and ethnology provide interesting examples of whom and what actions Apaches considered honorable. These codes often run against the grain of popular beliefs about the Apaches.

Blood revenge was an Apache matter of honor. It was the responsibility of relatives and friends of the one killed to take blood revenge on the killer. A son was expected to take blood revenge for a murdered father. There are many historic examples of this. Has-kay-bay-nay-ntayl (Brave and Tall and Will Come to a Mysterious End), also known as Apache Kid, began his downhill slide as a highly respected army scout to a desperado after he killed "Rip," the brother of "Gon-zizzie," who had murdered Kid's father, Toga-de-Chuz, a member of Capitan Chiquito's band of Aravaipa Apaches. Friends of Toga-de-Chuz quickly killed Gon-zizzie for the murder, but six months later, Apache Kid, believing Rip had convinced Gon-zizzie that he should kill Toga-de-Chuz, hunted Rip down and put a bullet through his heart.[3]

Killing during raids for livestock or supplies was frowned on. The Apaches wanted those they stole from to prosper so they could come back again and have more to steal. Mexican *hacendados* (wealthy landowners) understood this and left corrals of livestock (usually horses) for Apaches to take on their raids, so they would leave the rest of their property alone, and peons were not killed trying to defend livestock from the raid.

Killing in times of war was different from occasional killing during a raid. The Apaches asked no quarter and gave none. On a man-for-man basis, and equally armed, an Apache warrior was equivalent to at least ten army soldiers. An Apache child trained to be quiet, to be in the best physical shape his body could sustain, to fight well with all the tools at his command, and to suffer without complaint any pain or loss to win his battles and survive. Above all, an Apache was taught to value his independence and freedom, most of which was swept away by the tsunami of Anglo settlers from the East, who, with overpowering numbers and weapons, unlimited supplies, and nerves of steel, drove the Apaches onto reservations and exiled Geronimo and his people east for twenty-seven years as prisoners of war.

During Geronimo's last breakout in 1885/1886, the Apaches raided on both sides of the border. On the Mexican side, Geronimo killed anyone and everyone he could because he hated Mexicans for killing his aged mother, young wife, and three young children in a surprise attack around 1850 while the camp's men were away. But on the American side of the border, Geronimo's people also killed everyone they encountered in raids. During their prisoner of war captivity at Mount Vernon Barracks outside of Mobile, Alabama, General Crook asked Naiche, second son of Cochise and Geronimo's chief, why they killed everyone on the American side of the border during their raids. Naiche answered simply, "It was war." They believed they had to do it to ensure no survivors gave pursuers any information about them.

Within a few days after becoming the agent at San Carlos on August 8, 1874, John Clum made the first four hires for an Apache police force. Several weeks after the police began work, a Tonto chief, Des-a-lin, who regularly beat his wives, began tying the youngest wife to a tree and throwing knives at her for sport. She reported this to Clum, who publically embarrassed Des-a-lin for treating his wife that way. Des-a-lin thought about it for a few days and decided to put an end to Clum interfering in his personal business. He bought a pistol and went looking for the agent. Finding Clum in his office, Des-a-lin attempted to shoot him, but instead Des-a-lin was shot dead by his own brother, the police officer Taucelclyee. As Taucelclyee and Clum looked down at Des-a-lin's body, Taucelclyee absentmindedly stroked his still-smoking rifle and said, "I've killed my own chief and my own brother. But he was trying to kill you, and I'm a policeman. It was my duty." Clum had learned as had Tom Jeffords with Cochise, Al Sieber, General Crook's Chief of Scouts, and Capt. John Bourke, General Crook's Executive Officer, and many other southwestern frontiersmen, that to an Apache, honor was above all price.[4]

Apache Raiding and Warfare

There is a famous line in the John Wayne film *Fort Apache* where he says, "Well, if you saw them, Sir, they weren't Apaches." John C. Cremony, who was an army captain at Bosque Redondo, where the army kept the Mescaleros and Navajos penned up from 1863 to 1868, writes in *Life Among the Apaches* of an Apache warrior, Tats-ah-das-ay-go (Quick Killer), who, while they were on a great prairie dotted with a few shrubs and small bushes, demonstrated how well Apaches could conceal themselves. They stood by a small bush "hardly big enough to hide a rabbit." Quick Killer stood behind the bush and told Cremony to turn his back until Quick Killer told him he was ready. Instead, Cremony said he would walk forward until Quick Killer told him to stop. Quick Killer agreed, and Cremony, taking a quick look over his shoulder, quietly pulled his revolver and started walking forward. He hadn't taken more than ten steps when Quick Killer said he was ready. Cremony turned around and walked back to the bush. Quick Killer had disappeared. Cremony walked all the way around the bush three or four times, looked in every direction, and though there was nothing behind which to hide, the prairie was smooth and unbroken. It seemed as if the earth had just opened up and swallowed Quick Killer. Cremony called for Quick Killer to appear, and to Cremony's great surprise, Quick Killer stood up laughing from under thick grama grass within two feet of him and within six feet of the bush. He told Cremony that Apache children regularly practiced this game of "hide-and-seek," until they were "perfectly capable" of hiding like he had. "Hide-and-seek" was a fundamental skill learned by Apache warriors.

From an early age Apache boys and girls trained with bows and arrows and rock slings, and every day they ran short dash races and long distances. As they began approaching their maturity, the girls didn't play with the boys and stayed with other girls and their mothers learning what women needed to know to support their men and nurture their families. The boys continued to train with stronger bows and better arrows in games where they shot at any and everything, including each other, or if winners in target shooting contests, they collected the arrows used by their competitors. They fought mock battles with slings and rocks where bones might be broken and eyes lost, and they physically trained to the point where they could run long distances across the desert. They had the strength and stamina to outrun a horse over long distances or could suffer nearly any privation to overcome an enemy.

Although the Apaches were the first to steal horses from the Spaniards, they never became horse-mounted fighters (cavalry) like the plains tribes such as the Comanche, Sioux, Kiowa, or Cheyenne. Apaches were, in fact, mounted infantry. They rode horses to carry loads and for fast getaways, but in fights, they usually dismounted and fought on foot rather than from horseback. Ambush (as might be judged from Henry Farny's numerous paintings of Apache ambush settings) was their favorite form of attack—quick and deadly with little personal exposure. The Apaches saw the effectiveness and quickly adapted to *Indah* (White Man) rifles because their range was much greater than a bow and arrow, but even into the 1880s, they still carried bows that were often faster and deadlier than *Indah* firearms for in-close fights. For the Apache, the problem in using firearms was keeping and finding enough ammunition of which the *Indah* seemed to have an unlimited supply.

Apache Warrior Women

VICTORIO'S SISTER LOZEN, AN UNMARRIED WARRIOR AND *DI-YEN* (MEDICINE WOMAN), was unknown to American history until the narrator of *In the Days of Victorio*, James Kaywaykla, nephew of Lozen, first told Eve Ball about her.[1] Respected historians have questioned whether she existed and called Lozen a myth while others firmly agree with Eve Ball.[2]

Apache Warrior Women On the Prisoner of War Train To Florida With Naiche and Geronimo, 1886

Lozen

Dah-tes-te

Naiche — Geronimo

Apache warrior women Lozen and Dah-tes-te with Naiche and Geronimo beside the Apache Florida-bound prisoner of war train, 1886. This is the only photograph believed to be that of Lozen, and some historians dispute even this picture.
PHOTO COURTESY OF NATIONAL ARCHIVES, 530797

Lozen was born in the 1840s, probably in the Warm Springs area of southwestern New Mexico, and was about twenty years younger than Victorio.[3] Her name meant "little sister." Like all Apache girls, Lozen trained along with boys. The girls were encouraged to develop their physical strength, learn how to mount unsaddled horses without help, become proficient in archery and rock-slinging skills, learn to hunt and stalk game, and learn different ways to escape enemies. Many girls rivaled the fastest boys in footraces, and girls and young women were expected to guard the camp and fight off attackers when the men were gone.

Kaywaykla told Eve Ball, "Much has been written of the low regard in which Indian women were held. Among my people that was not true. Instead they were respected, protected, and cherished." Lozen could outrun the men and ride like the wind. She was handy with bow and rifle, but the men didn't resent her. "They were frankly proud of her and her ability. Above all they respected her integrity." It's likely that Lozen rode with Nana on his raid in the fall of 1881 to avenge the death of Victorio. That raid covered over a thousand miles, killed up to fifty people, and captured two hundred horses and mules although the Apaches were pursued by more than a thousand soldiers and three hundred civilians.

Lozen's gift of Power was her ability to divine the location of the enemy. She would stand with outstretched arms, palms up, and pray. While turning slowly, her hands would tingle and the palms would change color when they pointed toward the enemy. The closer the enemy came, the more vivid the feeling.

Many young men asked Victorio for permission to marry her, but Lozen begged him not to order her to marry and said she would never take a husband. Victorio assumed she hadn't met the man of her choice. She became friends with Dah-tes-te, another female fighter who accompanied her husband, Anandiah, and spent three years fighting the Americans with Geronimo. According to Charlie Smith, who was a young Mescalero boy abducted with his mother and two other women by Geronimo's men, Dah-tes-te was a very good shot and absolutely fearless. Both Lozen and Dah-tes-te were often used as Geronimo's messengers.

The army ignored Apache fighting women because soldiers held "squaws" in low regard. John C. Cremony, an army captain at Bosque Redondo during the early years of Apache captivity, chided his fellow officers as early as 1868 for failing to recognize Apache women for their fighting ability and numbers. "Many of the women . . . ride like centaurs and handle their rifles with deadly skill . . . In the estimate made, no account is taken of fighting women, who are numerous, well trained and desperate, often exhibiting more real courage than the men."

Lozen and Dah-tes-te surrendered to the army along with Geronimo's other warriors in 1886. Lozen died of tuberculosis at Mount Vernon Barracks in Alabama in 1890. Dah-tes-te survived tuberculosis and pneumonia, divorced Anandiah, later married Coonie, and, after her release as a prisoner of war, moved to the Mescalero Reservation. She died at a very old age at White Tail on the reservation in 1955.

1861 Apache Diplomacy on the El Paso Road

THE CIVIL WAR BEGAN IN APRIL 1861 WITH THE CONFEDERACY FIRING ON FORT SUMter. In Texas the Confederacy moved quickly to take New Mexico and Arizona with the strategy of then marching north to take the Colorado silver mines. Early in July, Lt. Col. John R. Baylor and the Second Texas Mounted Rifles arrived in El Paso. Marching to El Paso, Baylor, who believed Apaches were vermin to be exterminated, posted companies of his regiment at the forts along the road from San Antonio. The Mescalero bands of Nicolás and Antonio took advantage of the war between the whites and were a major threat to shipping, cattle herds, and ranches around Fort Davis on the western side of the Davis Mountains.

Attack on the Stagecoach, painting by Herman W. Hansen, 1902, is representative of the harassment of the stage lines on the San Antonio–El Paso road near the Guadalupe and Davis Mountains.

Patrick McCarthy, the sutler (one who sold provisions to the soldiers from a mercantile store on post) and postmaster at Fort Davis, hit upon the idea of making the Apaches allies with the Confederacy against the Union bluecoats. He persuaded Nicolás to visit Fort Davis under a flag of truce and told him that the head soldier chief in El Paso would welcome him like a brother, make a great feast, have a smoke, and make a treaty. Nicolás's natural reluctance to get close to the enemy was overcome by his need to show his courage. The next morning McCarthy and Nicolás boarded a stage for El Paso about 170 miles to the northwest. It was the first and only time the stage line made the run to El Paso without fearing attack by Apaches.

At Fort Bliss, near El Paso, Nicolás was received like a king. Colonel Baylor, McCarthy, and a wealthy landowner, James Magoffin, held a big formal banquet for him and each gave a speech that expressed how much they admired and wanted Nicolás to be their brother. When the whites finished speaking, Nicolás said with a straight face, "I am glad I have come. My heart is full of love for my pale-face brothers. They have not spoken with a forked tongue. When I lie down at night, the treaty will be in my heart, and when I arise in the morning, it will still be there. And I will be glad I am at peace with my pale-face brothers. I have spoken."

The next day Nicolás and McCarthy climbed in a stage that Baylor had loaded with gifts. Baylor and Magoffin wished Nicolás a safe trip home and pledged again their desire for friendship. Nicolás again pledged his eternal friendship, and the stage headed south. The trip back was quiet, and McCarthy dozed in his seat. As the stage approached Barrel Springs, Nicolás leaned over, jerked McCarthy's revolvers from their holsters, and vaulted out of the coach to hit the ground running, soon to be lost in the brushy sea of creosotes, mesquite, ocotillo, and yucca while McCarthy bellowed curses after him.

Soon after Nicolás escaped the stage, he and his warriors stole a herd of cattle near Fort Davis and lured an army patrol chasing them into an ambush that wiped out the entire detachment. It was the start of a new season of raiding and torture horrors on the road to El Paso.

"My Father Was a Good Man; He Killed Lots of White Eyes"

THE GREAT NEDNHI APACHE CHIEF JUH (PRONOUNCED WHOA) WAS, BY APACHE STANDARDS, tall (about six feet in height) and heavyset (about 225 pounds). He married Geronimo's sister, Ishton, who after a birth that nearly killed her, gave him Daklugie, the youngest of his three sons. Delzhinne was his eldest son. Daklegon was the middle son, and each son was born from a different wife. Ishton also had a daughter, Jacali, by Juh.

Juh's stronghold was high on a flat-topped mountain about halfway between Janos and Casas Grandes on the east side of the Sierra Madre in the Mexican state of Chihuahua. The Mexican army of Porfirio Díaz attempted to storm this stronghold several times but quit after growing tired of eating boulders the Apaches rolled down on them.

The Nednhi were the fiercest of Apache warriors. Dan Thrapp, the great Apache wars historian, says that after Victorio, Juh was the ablest chief and warrior, but that his fame was mainly among his own people, while for the Mexicans and Anglos it was hidden by the flood of stories and reports about his brother-in-law, Geronimo. Stories told about Juh illustrate his arrogance, vision, supreme ability, and self-assurance. One story describes how Mexicans captured Nednhi women and children to work as mine slaves when they were on the *llano* (dry prairie) cutting mescal. It took Juh a while to find where they had been taken, and his warriors watched the village for an opportunity to take them back. The Apaches soon learned nearly the entire village went to a brown robe (Catholic priest) ceremony every seven days, leaving only a few guards for the slaves. One Sunday the Apaches quietly killed the guards and freed their women and children. Then they blocked the church doors so those inside couldn't get out. The night before, Fun, Geronimo's half brother, had dug a small hole in the roof at the back of the church. After Apaches blocked the doors, he ignited a chili bomb (hot chili pods mixed with wood shavings and pine sap), dropped it through the hole in the roof, and covered the hole with a blanket. The burning chili produced a smoke more toxic than tear gas, and soon those inside were begging to be set free. The Apaches didn't open the doors, and all inside perished. As they

Asa Daklugie, youngest son of Juh, nephew of Geronimo, ca. 1953
PHOTO COURTESY OF LYNDA SÁNCHEZ/EVE BALL COLLECTION

left the village, the Apaches started landslides from the canyon walls surrounding the town and buried most of it.[1]

Another story tells of the Mexican town of Janos asking for peace with Juh and offering to provide the Apaches supplies when they needed them if they wouldn't raid around Janos. Juh agreed. When the Apaches were invited to celebrate with a few drinks of whiskey, their taste for the whiskey led them to drink too much. When they passed out drunk, the waiting Mexicans killed about half of them before the rest managed to get away.

Juh took his revenge. When the Mexicans proposed the same deal a few years later, Juh let only half his warriors go into town for their whiskey and made sure the Mexicans understood that half of his warriors, deadly sober, waited in their camp outside the village. Needless to say, no Apaches were killed at celebrations after that.

Juh died in October 1883 when his horse unexpectedly tumbled over a bank on the Río Aros. The water was waist deep and Daklugie, who was then about twelve, and Delzhinne rushed to get his head above water, but he was unconscious. No one knows if Juh had a heart attack or was injured when he fell. Delzhinne rode for help while Daklugie held Juh's head above water.

Shortly after Delzhinne and other warriors returned, Juh, who never regained consciousness, died. The warriors scraped out a grave on the west bank of Río Aros and, wrapping Juh in his blanket, buried him there. Three years later, Daklugie, who rode with the bands of Geronimo and Mangas, surrendered with the little band of Mangas six weeks after Geronimo surrendered, was made a prisoner of war and sent to the Carlisle Indian School in 1886. After twenty-seven years as a prisoner of war, Daklugie helped his people decide to leave Fort Sill, Oklahoma, for permanent homes on the Mescalero Reservation in New Mexico.[2]

Juh's Assassination of Lt. Howard Cushing

HISTORIANS HAVE LONG DEBATED IF JUH, THE GREAT NEDNHI APACHE CHIEF, WAS behind the ambush and assassination of Lt. Howard Cushing in May 1871. Many historians have argued that the chief who directed the ambush was Cochise. However, cavalry survivors of the ambush described the chief who directed it as being big and heavyset, the way Juh is often described, and the Apaches said Juh was responsible for the ambush of Lieutenant Cushing.[1] This is the story.

Captain John Bourke, General Crook's Executive Officer, writes in *On the Border with Crook* that the fighting with Cochise had not been going well in 1870. Lieutenant Howard Cushing, of the Third Cavalry, F Company, was stationed at Camp Grant. He was convinced that killing Cochise would end the Chiricahua war and killed any Apaches he came upon. Bourke called Cushing a "gallant" officer, which was cavalry speak for being fearless to the point of foolhardiness, and he didn't hesitate to risk the lives of his men as well as his own. According to Bourke, Cushing "had killed more savages of the Apache tribe than any other officer or troop of the United States Army had done before or since."

The story of Lieutenant Cushing's assassination begins when a few Mescalero families in New Mexico left the Sacramento Mountains to camp and hunt in the Guadalupe Mountains on the New Mexico–Texas border. One afternoon the Mescalero men returned from a hunt to find all in the camp killed except for two women, both wounded in a leg, all victims of an attack led by Lieutenant Cushing. According to Daklugie, Juh had heard much about Lieutenant Cushing and his attacks on Apache camps in Arizona. After learning what had happened to the Mescaleros, Juh was determined to kill Cushing and had scouts out watching for him after he returned to Arizona. Cushing continued attacking Apache camps around Camp Grant and Globe, Arizona, and it was several months before Juh had an opportunity to retaliate fully. In the interim, Juh's warriors had three skirmishes with Cushing but were unable to inflict any damage.

In early May 1871, Juh finally managed to maneuver Lieutenant Cushing into an ambush west of Tombstone. Juh had one of his women lead a horse up a canyon to Bear Springs in the Whetstone Mountains so Cushing's soldiers would follow her. Cushing

My Bunkie, displayed at the Metropolitan Museum of Art. Soldiers fought hard to save each other during attacks, such as Juh's on Lieutenant Cushing. (Painting by Charles Schreyvogel, 1899)
COURTESY OF METROPOLITAN MUSEUM OF ART

crossed her trail and sent old, experienced sergeant John Mott and three men to follow her while he continued on the main trail with the detachment that included a mule train with supplies. Sergeant Mott and his men followed the trail for three quarters of a mile until it turned into another canyon not much more than a deep, sandy arroyo. Mott realized the woman was taking care to leave clear prints, even avoiding stepping on rocks she might have used to make the trail disappear. He decided they were being led into a trap and led his men up the side of the arroyo, from where he saw about fifteen Apaches in a side canyon that would have cut off their retreat had they continued following the woman's trail. He sent one man after Lieutenant Cushing believing that, with his position and arms, he and the other two troopers could hold off the fifteen Apaches until Cushing returned. After Sergeant Mott and the two troopers dismounted, he saw a second and much larger group of Apaches to their left running to get behind his position. Sergeant Mott decided to remount and retreat. The Apaches fired a volley at Sergeant Mott and the two troopers, severely wounding one and disabling the horse of another. The trooper who had signaled Lieutenant Cushing saw what was happening and fired into the advancing Apaches, making them think the main body was coming up and pause long enough to give Mott and the other two time to escape to cover. The Apaches armed with breech-loading rifles tried to keep the troopers pinned down while others crept forward in an attempt to take them alive.

Lieutenant Cushing arrived with the rest of the troop and made ready to advance on the Apaches with eleven men, despite the warning from Sergeant Mott and a civilian mule train packer that they were outnumbered by at least eleven to one and should retreat. Lieutenant Cushing made fun of their concerns and went forward. He was soon shot in the chest, and as Sergeant Mott dragged him back to cover, Cushing was hit in the head and instantly killed. Sergeant Mott managed to get the rest of the men out of the canyon, and the Apaches, seeing Lieutenant Cushing had been killed, let them go. Daklugie said the killing of Cushing was Juh's proudest moment.

Victorio

Kaywaykla rode with Nana and Victorio, who gave him his name, when he was a young boy. He and his mother were among the seventeen survivors who escaped being captured or wiped out with Victorio at Tres Castillos in Mexico south of El Paso, Texas, in October 1880.[1] The story of Nana's raid in 1881 after Victorio was wiped out is told in part 1, chapter 7, "Nana, Victorio's Segundo."

Most historians believe Victorio was born in 1825 and grew to manhood in the Warm Springs area of the Black Range near Ojo Caliente in New Mexico. He belonged to the Warm Spring Apache band that was also known as Mimbreños by the Mexicans and by other Apaches as Chihenne (Red People) for the red stripe of clay they wore across their faces. Victorio's people were first united under the great chief Mangas Coloradas (Red Sleeves) around 1837. By the time Victorio was in his early to mid-twenties, he had become a major warrior with great tactical skills who, along with Nana and Geronimo, led bands of thirty to fifty warriors on many successful raids into northern Mexico. His famous sister, Lozen, the great warrior and medicine woman, came to be one of his primary advisors. He is believed to have been the son-in-law of Mangas Coloradas, who unified the Apaches by marrying his daughters to powerful leaders. Cochise also married a daughter of Mangas Coloradas, which made Cochise and Victorio brothers-in-law.

In 1862 Victorio joined Mangas Coloradas in a successful war to drive miners off Apache land and away from the Santa Rita del Cobre copper mines in southwestern New Mexico Territory. Near the same time Victorio joined Cochise in his war against the Americans after Second Lt. George Nicholas Bascom hanged Cochise's brother and two nephews. This occurred soon after Cochise slashed his way out of Bascom's tent during their first parley when Bascom demanded Cochise turn over Felix Ward (later to be known as a famous scout, Mickey Free), a child he believed Cochise had taken in a raid. Cochise claimed innocence and asked for a few days to learn who had the boy. Bascom refused and said he would hold Cochise and the people with him prisoner until the boy was returned. After his escape, Cochise took his own prisoners to trade for those whom

Victorio, protégé and probable son-in-law of Mangas Coloradas, strong and vigorous, was the model Apache warrior. *Apache Warrior*, by C. M. Russell, 1907.

Bascom held. Misunderstandings in the dickering to trade prisoners led Cochise to kill his prisoners and Bascom retaliated by hanging Cochise's male relatives.

Mangas Coloradas was murdered by U.S. Army guards in mid-January of 1863 after he came to attend what he believed would be negotiations for a treaty that would let the Mimbreños have their own reservation near Warm Springs. With Mangas Coloradas gone, Victorio became chief and continued his support of Cochise in his war against the Americans.

In 1872 Cochise decided to end his war and accept a reservation in the Dragoon Mountains of Arizona managed by his friend Tom Jeffords. Victorio had already accepted a reservation at Ojo Caliente two years earlier. The reservation worked well for the Mimbreños, but in 1872 the government decided to move them to a new reservation, Tularosa, about seventy miles to the northwest. In the summer of 1874, that reservation closed and the Mimbreños were allowed to return to Ojo Caliente. In 1877 John Clum, agent at San Carlos, arrested Geronimo at Ojo Caliente and, following orders from the Department of Interior, which was implementing the government's Policy of Consolidation, moved the Mimbreños to San Carlos in late April to early May. Compared to Ojo Caliente, San Carlos was a hellhole of insufferable heat, mosquitoes, snakes, dust, and disease. In early September, Victorio broke out of San Carlos with about three hundred Mimbreños mounted on ponies they had stolen from the White Mountain Apaches. The next morning, tribal police and White Mountain volunteers left San Carlos and quickly trapped Victorio's people against a tall cliff in the Natanes Mountains and recaptured their stock and that of Victorio. The pursuers didn't have enough firepower to overrun Victorio's position and returned to San Carlos. Soon they regrouped, began the chase again, and caught up with the Mimbreños at Ash Creek, where Victorio lost a few of his men and about thirty women and children. That night he managed to slip away and stole mounts from nearby ranches, but he killed as few *Indah* as possible in the hopes of returning to Ojo Caliente. After numerous skirmishes that cost Victorio more than fifty dead, nearly two hundred of his people—Victorio not among them—surrendered at Fort Wingate. Since the other bands back at San Carlos would never have accepted the Mimbreño horse thieves, they were taken to Ojo Caliente, where Victorio soon appeared. General Hatch, commanding the New Mexico Department, promised that he would use his influence to let the Mimbreños stay if they behaved themselves. They waited nearly a year from the fall of 1877 to the summer of 1878 and were on their best behavior. Finally, with the army forcing the issue with the Department of Interior, the decision was made to return the Mimbreños to San Carlos, and two companies of scouts and regular troopers showed up to escort them back. Victorio was enraged and fled to the mountains in August of 1878 with about eighty followers, most warriors. His band soon grew to more than one hundred.

It was an unusually wet fall, and even the Apache scouts trying to follow Victorio's constantly washed-out trails couldn't find him. In December, under tight guard, about 170

Mimbreños, those not escaping with Victorio, were returned to San Carlos. However, at about the same time, Nana, with sixty-three old men, women, and children, appeared at the Mescalero agency and asked to be taken in. The agent, Fred C. Godfroy, was happy to have them. They camped in a Rinconada canyon. However, Nana failed to tell Godfroy that a number of young warriors who came separately over the mountains would join him in that camp. Since they weren't numbered in Godfroy's count, they could come and go as they pleased. In February of 1879, Victorio and his men, wanting their families returned to Ojo Caliente, begged the officer in charge for them to be sent anywhere except San Carlos. In April, word came that the Mimbreños would be located at Mescalero. On hearing this, Victorio thought better of his earlier plea and took off again. However, he showed up at Mescalero with thirteen warriors in June and declared he wanted to be on the reservation. Through an unfortunate coincidence and Godfroy's poor management and bureaucratic ineptitude in refusing to supply food to the starving Indians until he received approval from his superiors at the Bureau of Indian Affairs, Victorio became convinced that he was about to be taken prisoner and broke out of Mescalero in early September, and all the misery of the Victorio War began.

In October of 1880, Victorio, running low on ammunition and evading American and Mexican army units south of El Paso, sent Nana and thirty warriors to find more ammunition and to hunt while the rest of his band camped at Tres Castillos in Chihuahua. A Mexican army contingent under Col. Joaquín Terrazas happened to be at the right place at the right time and attacked Victorio at Tres Castillos. The Mexicans wiped out sixty warriors and eighteen women and children. Seventy women and children were captured and sold as slaves in Chihuahua. Victorio's lack of ammunition is clear from the fact that Terrazas lost three men killed. Seventeen women and children, including Kaywaykla and his mother, managed to escape. Some claim that Victorio was shot and killed by a Tarahumara Indian named Mauricio, who was awarded a nickel-plated rifle and three thousand dollars. However, Geronimo, Daklugie, and other Apaches who had spoken to survivors of the massacre say that when Victorio fired his last bullet at the enemy, knowing all was lost, he stabbed his heart rather than be taken.

A Victorio Cavalry Ambush

VICTORIO AND NANA LEFT THE MESCALERO RESERVATION WHEN A BUMBLING AGENT, S. A. Russell, refused to give Victorio's Mimbreño Apaches rations until Washington bureaucrats approved it. Victorio's warriors were hungry. Dr. Blazer, who ran the sawmill on the reservation, had already provided the Mimbreños beef and corn out of his own supplies, but Russell wouldn't budge. Around September 1, 1879, Victorio stormed into Russell's office and dragged him around by his long gray beard, demanding his promised

Victorio's cavalry ambush was similar to action depicted in *The Advance Guard*, by Fredrick Remington, ca. 1890, on display at the Chicago Art Institute.

COURTESY OF ART RESOURCE/ART INSTITUTE OF CHICAGO

rations. But after deciding it was useless to bully Russell, he went and shook Blazer's hand, thanked him for his help, and led his warriors, along with a few Mescaleros who joined them, out of the reservation. On the way out of Temporal Canyon at the foot of the Sacramento Mountains, they killed a couple of sheepherders and took their horses even before they left the reservation. Victorio's group headed west through the San Andres Mountains, across the Jornada del Muerto and Río Grande, and into the Gila country of the Black Range, killing and burning as they went. Then he swung south on a route that took him across the New Mexico border into Texas and down into the Big Bend country and then back across the Río Grande into the state of Chihuahua in Mexico.

General Hatch, directing the army's chase of Victorio, picketed every cavalry troop he could command, ready to ride with tough, battle-tested commanders, at positions along the New Mexico and eastern Arizona borders waiting for Victorio to come north. On September 4, 1879, Victorio suddenly appeared at the Ojo Caliente cavalry post about sixty miles north of the mining town of Hillsboro, and far behind Hatch's line of waiting troopers facing south.

At Ojo Caliente, eight privates herded forty-six horses on a hot and dusty range where there was little grass after an eighteen-month drought. The men, staying within sight of the post, were attacked without warning when Victorio and sixty warriors appeared. In five minutes, all the herders had been killed and the horses had disappeared in a cloud of dust.

Two weeks later, on September 18, in the rough country near the headwaters of Animas Creek, less than six miles south of Hermosa on Palomas Creek, at the junction of a side canyon and Animas Creek Canyon, Victorio laid a deadly ambush for a cavalry patrol searching for him. Captain Byron Dawson and forty-six Navajo scouts and Buffalo Soldiers of the Ninth Cavalry were, according to the *Silver City Herald*, "hardly aware of [the Apache's] immediate presence before [he] could extricate himself without heavy loss and perhaps utter destruction." Victorio had about 150 of his fighting men positioned on the walls of the canyon, and they poured a rain of hell down on Captain Dawson's command. The troopers scattered, letting their terrified horses go, but the Apaches had most of the available cover under fire. Captain Dawson sent a rider racing for help. Around ten o'clock, Capt. Charles D. Beyer, leading fifty-two men, many of them civilians from Hillsboro across the mountains about fourteen miles to the southwest, charged in to help Captain Dawson. The Apaches kept up a withering fire that made it impossible to counterattack. Captain Beyer could only hope to provide enough covering fire to keep Captain Dawson's command out of the death trap Victorio was trying to close.

The fight lasted all day, with many acts of heroism by the trapped troopers. Second Lt. Matthias W. Day, against orders, carried a wounded trooper across two hundred yards of space under heavy fire and was awarded the Medal of Honor by Congress, even though Captain Beyer wanted to court-martial him.

As the sun was setting, Captain Beyer withdrew and left the field to Victorio. According to Apache historian Dan Thrapp, eight men, including a civilian and two Navajo scouts, were killed and two enlisted men were seriously wounded. Fifty-three government horses and mules were abandoned, thirty-two were reported killed, and much of the officers' baggage and other booty was left to the Apaches. It is believed that Victorio didn't lose a single warrior.

By this time, 150 men eager to wipe out Victorio were on the way from Hillsboro and the Black Range country. Victorio paused long enough to pick off eighteen of them and then rode on. It would be another year of raids and battles before Victorio, out of bullets and men and under attack by the Mexican army under Col. Joaquín Terrazas, stabbed himself in the heart at Tres Castillos on October 14, 1880, and ended a long trail of blood.

Nana, Victorio's Segundo

NANA WAS VICTORIO'S SEGUNDO (NUMBER TWO OR SECOND-IN-COMMAND) AND SON-IN-law, although he was about twenty-five years older than Victorio. They were Mimbreño Apaches (also known as Warm Springs Apaches or the Chihenne People for the red stripe of clay they wore on their faces), who with their people were ordered from their desired reservation in the Cañada Alamosa, a valley in central New Mexico near Ojo Caliente (Warm Springs), in May 1877 and sent to San Carlos Reservation. In September 1877, three hundred Mimbreños under Victorio left San Carlos to live wild and free.

Apparently parting company with Victorio in December 1878, Nana appeared at the Mescalero agency with sixty-two old men, women, and children. The agent, Fred C. Godfroy, welcomed them with open arms and gave them ration passes. Sly Nana didn't show or register his warriors with Godfroy, but rather had them come over the mountains alone to join them where he and the others camped hidden in Rinconada Canyon on the reservation. This meant the warriors could come and go as they pleased, and Godfroy would never know the difference. Nana used his warriors to stay in constant contact with Victorio, who continued to roam free.

In July 1879, Victorio decided to settle on the Mescalero Reservation, where it appeared Nana's people were treated well and his people would be allowed to stay. However, agent Russell would not give Victorio and his warriors rations until approval came from Washington. Victorio was not happy with Russell's delay and was concerned that he was somehow being tricked to stay at the agency until the army came for him. Spooked by word that a Silver City grand jury had indicted him for murder and horse theft, and then seeing a hunting party including a judge and prosecuting attorney cross the reservation, he thought they had come for him, and then later he heard a bugle call from approaching cavalry for which a frightened Russell had sent.

Victorio left the reservation with his own Mimbreños and some Mescaleros and was later joined by Navajo and Comanche warriors to begin a war in southern New Mexico and Arizona and northern Mexico that lasted until October of 1880 when, running low on ammunition, he and eighty-six of his warriors were wiped out by Mexican general

Nana, Mimbreño Apache, photograph by Frank A. Randall, 1884
PHOTO COURTESY OF LIBRARY OF CONGRESS

Joaquín Terrazas at Tres Castillos. Nana, who was half-blind and hobbled by arthritis, had a special supernatural Power for finding ammunition, and he escaped slaughter by General Terrazas because, earlier in the day on October 14, 1880, Victorio had sent him and about thirty warriors to look for badly needed ammunition and to hunt.

After Victorio was wiped out, Nana disappeared. Some believe he went to Mexico, but James Kaywaykla, Nana's grandson, says Nana believed the Mexicans expected him to show up around Casas Grandes and were waiting for him. Instead, he went north and wintered in the Mogollon Mountains in southern Arizona. In the Season of Little Eagles (early spring), he went farther north and east to hide in the Sacramento Mountains in or near the Mescalero Reservation. He left the reservation area and moved out of the Sacramentos through Dog Canyon on July 17, 1881, with forty Mescaleros who had joined his original band of thirty. Although he was old and arthritic, Nana could ride seventy miles a day, and he was a brilliant military strategist. In the six weeks that most of his raid raged, seventy-four-year-old Nana covered over a thousand miles, fought eight battles with Americans and won them all, killed thirty to fifty enemies and wounded many more, captured two women and two hundred horses and mules, and eluded a thousand U.S. soldiers and three to four hundred civilians.

In early September 1881, Nana disappeared into the Sierra Madre, but he reappeared again to surrender along with Naiche, Geronimo, Chato, Loco, Chihuahua, and others to General Crook during his Sierra Madre campaign in May/June of 1883. When Geronimo broke out of San Carlos again in 1885, Nana went with him and others, but he surrendered in 1886 to become a prisoner of war in Florida. In his 1886 agreement with the Apaches, General Crook had said Nana, because of his age, didn't have to go to Florida, and the Chiricahuas only had to stay two years. But General Sheridan, Commander of the Army, angry because Crook had trusted Geronimo to come in on his own but had instead broke away again, countermanded Crook's orders, allowed Crook to resign, and replaced him with Gen. Nelson Miles, who shipped all the Chiricahuas, including those enrolled as government scouts, to St. Augustine, Florida, or in the case of Geronimo's little breakaway band, to Fort Pickens in Pensacola Bay, Florida. Conditions were so bad at St. Augustine that many Apaches died, and the Chiricahuas were sent to Mount Vernon Barracks, Alabama, in 1887 and 1888. In the fall of 1894, they were transferred to the military reservation at Fort Sill, Oklahoma, where they established homes, gardens, and villages. Nana died at Fort Sill in 1896.

Geronimo and the Arroyo Fight

GENERAL CROOK WENT INTO THE SIERRA MADRE IN 1883 WITH NEARLY TWO HUN-dred Apache scouts and fifty mounted troopers to bring back nearly seven hundred Apaches, including those who had been led or forced off the San Carlos Reservation by Geronimo, Naiche, Juh, et al., in late 1881 and early 1882. The original group leaving the reservation included seventy-four warriors and their women and children. Seven months later, in April 1882, this group met in council with Nana at the foot of Juh's mountain stronghold on the eastern side of the Sierra Madre west of Janos in Chihuahua. Led by Juh and Geronimo, the council decided that Loco and his Mimbreño people numbering about one hundred warriors and about three to four hundred women and children had to be rescued, even if they had to be forced, from the squalor, disease, and starvation at their camp between the Gila and San Carlos Rivers three miles east of the San Carlos agency.[1]

Several times in the winter of 1881/1882, Geronimo and Juh sent word to Loco that he should leave San Carlos and join them in the Sierra Madre. Loco wouldn't budge. In the early morning of April 19, 1882, Loco's people saw a line of armed warriors between them and the agency and others on horses coming across the river. One of the leaders yelled, "Take them all! . . . Shoot down anyone who refuses to go with us! Some of you men lead them out."

Loco's people were forced to follow on foot with little time to snatch up a few posses-sions, and Loco, at gunpoint, led them away with Geronimo in front. During the escape, the invaders killed two Apache policemen who rode to the camp to learn what was hap-pening. This convinced Loco's people that their safety depended on keeping quiet and not trying to escape their captors.

With short stops for rest, the group made it deep into the Gila Mountains to a ren-dezvous spot where they ate several hundred sheep the raiders had stolen and rested for two days. At this camp Loco was admitted to the council of leaders as they discussed plans to disappear into Mexico and escape the army troops scouring the country for them. It was clear that they had to make better time. After time on the reservation, most of Loco's people had grown soft and showed little of the speed and endurance of other

Fun and Geronimo, right, pose for a photograph by C. S. Fly at their meeting with General Crook, March 1886.
PHOTO COURTESY OF LIBRARY OF CONGRESS

Apaches trying to leave the reservation or escape their army pursuers. Several warriors were sent to raid ranches for horses. They took a day breaking them to ride and making reed saddles. Once mounted, the group began a night ride.

Lieutenant Colonel George A. Forsythe, with a superior force, searched for and ran into them in a rugged canyon near Stein's Peak, but was driven off, and the Apaches crossed the border into Mexico. Disregarding international law Forsythe continued the chase, caught them in camp on the Janos plains a few days later, and, after a day of fighting, again withdrew. The Apaches had lost fourteen men and most of their horses and supplies and had many wounded.

That night the survivors struggled on to a designated meeting place, but their path led straight into a trap set by Mexico's famous Indian fighter, Col. Lorenzo García, who had managed to learn the planned escape route from two of the raiders he had captured on the way to take Loco's people. By daylight, the escaping Apaches were walking in a long, irregular column about two miles long and running parallel to Aliso Creek, which was a dry streambed in a small arroyo. Warriors in the lead had stopped to rest and those in the column continued on, with another group of warriors in the rear guarding against another possible attack by the Americans.

García's men, who had hidden in a ravine, rushed the column from the side. They were quickly among the column shooting down women and children in all directions. The Apaches who were able ran and escaped to the mountains.

Geronimo called to the warriors to protect the women and children who had gathered around him for protection. Thirty-two warriors heeded his call and with Chihuahua made a stand in the dry arroyo. The arroyo was deep with an overhanging bank, and the women dug the gravel away and made holes in which they and the children could take cover. Scraping the sand away in the arroyo bottom, they had water, but it was soon mixed with blood. The men and women cut footholds in the arroyo banks so they could step up to fire at charge after charge of the Mexican soldiers who concentrated their fire there. It was a good defensive position, and the Apaches, skilled marksmen, shot down Mexican soldiers as soon as they appeared. James Kaywaykla, who was a young boy in the arroyo with his mother, said they could hear the Mexicans blow a bugle and their commander yell to his troops, "Go right in there and get Geronimo." Each time, the Apaches who understood Spanish warned the others to get ready, that a charge was coming again.

Fun, whose Apache name was Yahe-chul (Smoke Comes Out), became the real hero of the battle and thereafter was long remembered as a hero by his people. His half brother was Perico (White Horse), and his mother, Bonita, was first cousin to Geronimo. Fun was a big, strong man and at the time of the battle was about sixteen. When the soldiers blew their bugle and charged, Fun would pop up on top of the bank, run in a zigzag pattern toward the Mexicans using a trap-door, single-shot Springfield rifle, holding bullets between his fingers, reloading as he ran, and every time he fired, a soldier fell.

He did this three times as Chihuahua, lying on his side, covered him. Eugene Chihuahua said the bullets fired at his father came so close that the gravel they struck pitted Chihuahua's chest, making him look like he'd had smallpox. All this took place while Geronimo hid under the arroyo overhang with the women and children. Fun is said to have told Geronimo to get out and fight or he would shoot him. Geronimo and his son got out and escaped.

Loco was also a brave fighter. The Apaches in the arroyo were running out of ammunition. Fifty feet away, a mule that had been shot had a cowhide bag of cartridges on its pack frame. Loco tried to slip out and get the bag, but the Mexican fire was so hot he dropped the bag to get back under cover. A very old woman (another story says it was the warrior woman, Lozen) climbed over the bank, ran to the bag, and cut it free. It was too heavy for her to carry, so she dragged it back to the arroyo. As Fun drew the Mexicans' fire, he loaded cartridges over and over again from between his fingers while dodging from left to right. He managed to delay the charge long enough for the old woman to get within two or three steps of the bank's edge, where she fell with her feet toward the bank and was dragged feet first to safety still holding on to the bag of cartridges.

According to Kaywaykla, toward evening, with ammunition nearly gone and the warriors exhausted, Geronimo said, "Let's us men make a break. We could if we leave the women and children." Fun said, "Geronimo, if you say that again, I'm going to shoot you down right here."

The Mexicans formed for a last charge before it got too dark. The Apaches heard the bugle and the command to charge. Geronimo rallied to the fight. The soldiers got to the very edge of the arroyo and several fell there, but Fun shot the officer giving commands, and the soldiers retreated.

That night the Mexicans set the grass on fire to catch any Apaches trying to escape, but many did. The Apaches losses had been heavy, most lost during the opening of the ambush. Forsythe, who was there the next day, counted seventy-eight Apaches, three Mexican officers, and nineteen soldiers killed. Eleven of the Apaches were warriors. Thirty-three Apache women and children were captured, including Loco's daughter.

A year later, General Crook's campaign in the Sierra Madre to return the Apaches to San Carlos passed near the site of the battle. John Rope, a western Apache scout, visited the site and found many bleached-out bones, pieces of women's dresses, and lots of beads scattered on the ground.

By Geronimo's surrender in 1886, Fun was second in command. At Mount Vernon Barracks, he enlisted in the army along with Naiche and others. During his service, he shot his young wife, Belle, suspecting her of adultery. Fearing he would be hanged for murder, Fun shot himself. It was the first known case of suicide among the Chiricahua. Belle recovered and returned to her people. The debate over the reasons for Geronimo hiding at the arroyo battle continues.

Sierra Madre Apaches

THE APACHES CALLED THE SIERRA MADRE MOUNTAINS IN MEXICO THE "BLUE MOUN-tains." There were several bands of Apaches who called the Blue Mountains home, and in the early 1880s, the camp of the strongest chief belonged to Juh (pronounced Whoa), a Nednhi Chiricahua. Prior to 1883, the Apaches believed they were safe from attack by the U.S. Army bluecoats when they were in Mexico, and they made a number of camps in the mountains above Huachinera, a village on the Río Bavispe about eighty miles south of the United States–Mexico border. To the north of Juh's camp but below the border were a number of small camps scattered in the canyons of the Blue Mountains where water flowed, and some were even on island-like ridges where, up out of the dry heat and little water, big trees flourished from the more temperate climate and rain brought by clouds moving west to east, and there was abundant wild game.

Geronimo and Naiche left the San Carlos Reservation in September 1881, taking about eighty warriors with them and living at Juh's stronghold. They returned to San Carlos in April 1882 for Loco and his band and shepherded several hundred men, women, and children off the reservation down into Mexico. There, in the camps in the Blue Mountains, the warriors raided all over the states of Sonora and Chihuahua, leaving the San Bernardino and Bavispe Valleys desolate and Mexican people afraid to work their fields in the day or go out of their jacals at night.

General Crook made arrangements with the Mexican government to take his fighting men into the Sierra Madre and bring the Apaches back to San Carlos. In one of the most daring military operations in the last two hundred years, Crook led 50 soldiers and officers and 193 Apache scouts into Mexico around the first of May in 1883 to bring the Apaches back to San Carlos in a "good way." The Apache scouts were not mounted. They typically ran down the valleys and over the mountains tracking the reservation runaways. They could easily cover forty miles in a day and then would set up camps, where they waited for the slower-moving mounted soldiers and mule pack trains carrying supplies to catch up with them.

The Sierra Madre Apaches lived in deep canyons and on high mountains as illustrated in *Through the Pass*, by Henry Farny, ca. 1890, and carried on the last flickers of the Apache wars well into the twentieth century.

During the campaign, the scouts "mistakenly" attacked an Apache camp (believed to be that of Chief Bonito) in the Blue Mountains, but afterwards under Crook's watchful eye left the others alone. The Apaches living in the Sierra Madre were stunned and disheartened by the appearance of Crook and his scouts. Their own people, the scouts, seemed to have turned against them, and they concluded there was no place they could hide to get away from the bluecoats. Without any more fighting, the Apaches, including Geronimo, Chihuahua, Loco, Chato, and many other legendary warriors, returned to the misery of the San Carlos Reservation.

After Geronimo broke out a third time and then finally surrendered to General Miles on September 4, 1886, no one knows how many Apaches stayed behind in hidden camps in the Blue Mountains or how many renegades and bandits, north or south, camped and worked with them. However, we know these phantoms had a number of camps, although they were relatively small. We know records exist that describe their attacks on travelers across the high mountain trails well into the twentieth century. We know of Apache children in the little camps wiped out by Mexican raiders being taken in by Mexican families as late as 1930 and later adopted, and we know of stone shelters in abandoned Sierra Madre Apache camps that Grenville Goodwin discovered in the 1930s, and his son Neil found others in the mid-1990s. The Apache wars, in fact, continued well into the twentieth century. There is evidence to suggest that great-grandchildren of the Sierra Madre Apaches may still live in the high Blue Mountains.

The Geronimo Wars

Geronimo broke out of the San Carlos Reservation three times to begin new wars against the Anglos and the Mexicans. The stories behind those breakouts tell much about the man and why the U.S. government so feared him that General Miles lied in order to coax him into surrendering and then exiled him and all the other Chiricahua seventeen hundred miles east as prisoners of war, ultimately to hold them for twenty-seven years. It was not until Geronimo died after twenty-three years in captivity that the government gave serious thought to the release of the Chiricahuas.[1]

Geronimo's Only Capture

John Clum, feisty, arrogant, college educated, honorable, able, and efficient, appeared as the San Carlos Indian agent on August 8, 1874. He was within two weeks of being twenty-three years old. He liked the Indians and, unlike most other agents, treated them fairly, and they responded in kind. By 1875, relations between the Apaches and Americans were at their most hopeful point since before the Civil War. However, this hope quickly evaporated when, in the same year, bureaucrats in charge of the Indian Office decided on a policy of "consolidation," where all the bands were to be taken off their reservations scattered across Arizona and New Mexico and consolidated at San Carlos. The consolidation policy was a recipe for disaster. Some bands didn't like each other, and this led to numerous fights. Some bands were forced to live in mosquito-infested areas along the Gila River, and cases of malaria developed that killed many. Smallpox also wiped out many and forced even friendly bands to live far apart from others. John Clum did not create the consolidation policy (although many Apaches believed that he did), but he enthusiastically carried it out.

In June of 1876, Clum was sent to bring the Chokonen Chiricahuas to San Carlos from the Apache Pass Reservation on the Arizona-Mexico border. This was the reservation to which General Howard and Cochise had agreed, and Tom Jeffords, at the insistence of Cochise, was agent. After Cochise died, Taza, his oldest son, who Cochise had groomed for leadership, became chief. Clum talked with Taza and Naiche, his brother, and they gave their consent to being moved. Jeffords told Clum a second band under Juh, Geronimo, and Nolgee had been included in the settlement with General Howard and wanted to talk with him. Clum met with them around June 7. Geronimo did the talking (Juh was chief but had a speech impediment that made him hard to understand by translators). He claimed they were willing to go to San Carlos but requested they leave to bring in their people about twenty miles away. Clum agreed but had Indian police shadow their return to their people.

Arriving at their camp, Juh, Geronimo, and Nolgee gave their followers orders to kill their dogs to prevent their barking, break camp, and disappear. It was the first breakout

Diablo, John P. Clum, and Eskiminzim at San Carlos, ca. 1875
PHOTO COURTESY OF NATIONAL ARCHIVES

from a reservation by Geronimo. By the time Clum's scouts reported what had happened, Juh, Nolgee, and Geronimo were long gone. Clum returned to San Carlos with 325 Chiricahuas under Taza. Juh and Nolgee took their people into strongholds in the Sierra Madre, but Geronimo and about forty followers appeared at the Warm Springs (Ojo Caliente) Reservation on July 21, 1876. Between the closing of the Chiricahua agency in June and the following October, this band had killed more than twenty people and taken 170 head of livestock.

On March 17, 1877, an army officer reported seeing Geronimo at the Ojo Caliente agency in New Mexico with about a hundred horses (he and about seven other leaders had stolen them from Pima Indians living near Tucson) and said that Geronimo was irate because he couldn't draw rations they had missed during their absence. On March 20, the commissioner of Indian Affairs sent Clum word to take his Indian police, arrest the renegades at Ojo Caliente, bring them to San Carlos, and hold them in confinement for murder and robbery.

Clum contacted the army for support and was told three companies of cavalry would meet him at Ojo Caliente on April 21. He took one hundred of his San Carlos Apache tribal police and, after riding over four hundred miles, arrived with an advance of twenty-two police on the evening of April 20. There, he received word that the cavalry would not arrive until April 22. He knew that if he waited, the "renegades" would vanish. He sent word that the rest of his police should come up during the night. Arriving about 4:00 a.m., they were concealed in an empty commissary warehouse. At daylight Clum sent word to Geronimo's camp summoning them to a conference. They came with their women and children not expecting a confrontation.

Clum, backed by six of his tribal police, faced off with Geronimo, and his seven fully armed "renegade" leaders gathered in a tight group in front of him. Clum accused them of killing men and stealing cattle and breaking their promise to come in to San Carlos the previous year. Now, he said he was going to bring them in.

Geronimo replied, "We are not going to San Carlos with you, and unless you are very careful, you and your Apache police will not go back to San Carlos either. Your bodies will stay here at Ojo Caliente to make food for coyotes."

Clum gave a prearranged signal. The commissary doors flew open and the hidden police rushed out. Geronimo and his warriors faced a potential crossfire between two lines of police holding a hundred cocked rifles. After some tense moments, including an Apache woman trying to take a pistol away from an American officer, Geronimo and his warriors laid down their rifles and other weapons as commanded. Clum marched them to the blacksmith shop and had them put in leg irons, riveted at the ankles and connected by chains, and then hauled them back to the guardhouse at San Carlos to stand trial for robbery and murder. This was the only time Geronimo was "captured."

Though John Clum once caught Geronimo through trickery, toward the end of his life, Geronimo took pleasure taunting the army, saying, "You have never caught me shooting."

Geronimo's First Breakout from San Carlos, 1878

As part of an Office of Indian Affairs reservation consolidation policy, in addition to Geronimo and his seven leaders, Clum was also ordered to bring Victorio and his Mimbreños back to San Carlos. The Mimbreños had lived in peace at Ojo Caliente for three years. It was their country. They had asked for it, and they wanted to stay. Victorio agreed to go after hearing the tribal police spread Clum's propaganda about San Carlos being a happy place, when in fact it was a nearly barren hellhole of heat, dust, mosquitoes, snakes, and disease and the army fighting with the Bureau of Indian Affairs over control and reservation policy.

After Clum took Geronimo and the others, the wagon train hauling the prisoners and Mimbreños took three weeks to reach San Carlos. Clum had Geronimo and the other shackled prisoners held in the San Carlos guardhouse until he could have them hanged. He had collected hearsay evidence about Geronimo's murders and thefts during his raids. The evidence came from hearing Apache gossip along the trail as he led the Mimbreños to San Carlos from Ojo Caliente. Clum wrote the Tucson sheriff that he had enough evidence to

San Carlos Reservation police and guardhouse, ca. 1880
PHOTO COURTESY OF LIBRARY OF CONGRESS

convict each of his eight shackled prisoners on many counts of murder and that the evidence should be used while the details were still fresh in the minds of his witnesses.

Geronimo had a clear understanding that this imprisonment "might easily have been death to me." It was to influence him the rest of his life. The White Eyes trying to catch him in later years never understood how strongly this event influenced his future flights. This fear was in addition to his deep-seated preference for the unlimited freedom of the old Apache lifeway, and the two together were the driving influences behind his surrenders, breakouts, and wars with the Americans.

Clum's arrogant personality saved Geronimo and the others from a preemptory trial and hanging. When Clum returned from Ojo Caliente, a company of soldiers was camped just outside the gates of the agency with orders to inspect and manage his Indians. The soldiers' orders were an example of the policy disputes then going on between the army and Bureau of Indian Affairs over who was in charge at San Carlos. In a fit of pique, Clum, without further ado, informed the commanding officer that he was in charge. Clum had already consolidated five Indian agencies in three years, saving the government $25,000 each year, and had grown in responsibility from originally supervising seven hundred to more than five thousand Indians. He fired off a telegram to the commissioner of Indian affairs at Washington and offered to take care of all the Apaches in Arizona if he was given two more companies of Indian police and a salary increase. The War Department threw a tantrum of its own when it learned of Clum's proposal. Trying to maintain some semblance of political balance with the War Department, the Indian Office rejected Clum's proposal, and upon receiving word of rejection of his proposal, Clum quit and left in a huff at the end of July 1877, neglecting to leave instructions about what to do with Geronimo and the others who sat shackled in the guardhouse.[1]

For reasons unknown, the Tucson sheriff procrastinated claiming and arresting Geronimo and the others after receiving Clum's note. Then, not long after Clum left, the new agent, Henry Lyman Hart, for reasons unknown except perhaps for lack of hard evidence against Geronimo and that the sheriff had not claimed them, removed their shackles and set them free. Geronimo was later to say in his autobiography, "After this, we had no more trouble with the tribal police, but I never felt at ease any longer at the Post [the agency]. We were allowed to live above San Carlos at a place now called Geronimo . . . All went well for a period of two years, but we were not satisfied."

After Clum left, weak and corrupt agents made things at San Carlos go from bad to worse. The Mimbreños, starving and in rags, dying from smallpox and sick from malaria caused by mosquitoes on the Gila flats, grew increasingly restive. Two Apache warriors who had ridden with Geronimo, Poinsenay, and Nolgee were successfully raiding in Mexico, and they snuck back on the reservation to make contacts with the Chiricahua to bring them out. On September 1, 1877, Poinsenay and his followers showed up at San Carlos rich with plunder from Mexico and bragging about successful raids. The next morning 22 women and children took off with Poinsenay, and Victorio and Loco left with 323 of their followers.

Geronimo did not go out with the Mimbreños, but dissatisfaction with the reservation continued to grow. Warriors began stealing guns and ammunition, and the women began stealing foodstuff in preparation for a breakout. Geronimo was one of the leaders to encourage it. Juh came up from Mexico to encourage it. One night Geronimo, drunk on *tiswin* (a mild corn beer), scolded his nephew for "no reason at all," and the nephew, probably the son of Nana and Geronimo's sister Nah-dos-te, took it so hard he committed suicide. Geronimo blamed himself for his nephew's death and, with Ponce and others who could not accept life on the reservation, left with Juh for his stronghold in the eastern Sierra Madre west of Casas Grandes, Mexico, on April 4, 1878.

In the fall of 1879, with the country aflame and up in arms fighting Victorio, making any raid highly dangerous and supplies hard to come by, Geronimo and Juh contacted General Willcox and asked him to be their friend, saying they had not been raiding with Victorio, didn't know where he was, and were willing to return to San Carlos. General Willcox agreed. After gathering their people, they showed up at San Carlos in December of 1879 or January of 1880.

Geronimo's Second Breakout from San Carlos, 1881

In May 1880, Victorio's son, Washington, led fourteen Victorio warriors to San Carlos to try to recruit Geronimo and Juh, but they were refused and driven away. A major manhunt for Victorio was then in play on both sides of the border. In September, plans were developed to recruit Juh's band to support General Willcox's operations to block and fight Victorio, but there is no evidence this ever would have succeeded. In October 1880, most of Victorio's band was wiped out at Tres Castillos in eastern Chihuahua. Only seventeen, including Nana, escaped. Juh and Geronimo's people continued to live quietly at San Carlos.

In July of 1881, Nana began a raid that lasted six weeks in retaliation for the massacre of Victorio. The raid ranged over a thousand miles, killed over fifty people, and wounded many more before Nana disappeared into the Sierra Madre. Geronimo and Juh's people on the reservation were not directly affected, but it drove government officials to make irrational decisions such as the disaster on Cibecue Creek that made the people hostile again.

For a variety of reasons, the Apaches began listening to the religious leader, Noch-ay-del-klinne, a "prophet," living on Cibecue Creek, who claimed he could commune with the spirits of the dead and even had the power to bring back to life their dead chiefs. He taught them a new dance that sent many into states of religious ecstasy. This happened while Nana was on his deadly raid, and it made those responsible for good order on the reservation exceptionally nervous, especially Joseph Capron Tiffany, the crooked agent who had been stealing supplies. In August 1881, Tiffany sent his Indian police to arrest the prophet, but they came back empty-handed and grumbling about white aggression. Even enlisted scouts attended the dances and came back converts. Rumors were flying among the Apaches that soldiers were planning to attack Noch-ay-del-klinne and his followers on Cibecue Creek and drive them from the reservation. In mid-August, Tiffany directed Col. Eugene Asa Carr at Fort Apache to "arrest or kill or both" the prophet. On August 29, Carr set out with 117 men, including 23 Apache scouts, to arrest the prophet, who quietly surrendered. However, his followers and some scouts defected and attacked Carr. The prophet, eighteen Apaches, and eight of Carr's men were killed. Daklugie, Juh's

Geronimo, at about age sixty, posing for Frank Randall at San Carlos in 1884, after returning from the 1881 breakout

PHOTO COURTESY OF LIBRARY OF CONGRESS

son, claimed Geronimo and Juh were there, but the army has no record of it. After their first angry reactions, the Apaches at San Carlos seemed to settle down.

General Willcox, anxious that a new Apache war might start, brought in twenty-two companies of soldiers (about twenty-two hundred officers, NCOs, and troopers) to keep order at San Carlos, and the reservation was overrun with soldiers. In mid-September 1881, Juh and Geronimo went to Tiffany to ask if the soldiers were there because of them and their past raids. Tiffany assured them they were not. Delighted, they shook hands and went back to their subagency. However, two White Mountain bands under Bonito with five warriors and George with twenty-two warriors had been involved in the fighting with Carr. They surrendered on September 25 and were paroled by General Willcox, but five days later, it was decided to take them into custody. On September 30, which was ration day for the reservation, three companies of cavalry suddenly appeared at the ration distribution. The two White Mountain bands on parole under Bonito and George to be taken back into custody fled to the Chiricahuas (their chief was Naiche, but Geronimo was the lead warrior) and Nednhis (their chief was Juh). Juh and Geronimo, along with the peaceful Naiche, fled with seventy-four warriors and their families and Bonito and his warriors for Mexico. Even George got away, but he ran in the opposite direction.

The army officers were baffled by the breakout. Geronimo and Juh's subagent, Ezra Hoag, said they were scared away, and even the Geronimo-hating Clum agreed. Early in the following year, April 1882, Geronimo led a successful war party back to San Carlos to force Loco and his people to return with them to the Sierra Madre.

After leaving San Carlos nearly all the raids the Apaches made were in Mexico, but in the fall of 1882, they raided southern Arizona for ammunition and horses. The raids in Arizona were enough for the War Department to order General Crook back from the plains wars to the military district of Arizona and New Mexico to take charge of the reservations.

General Crook met with the chiefs remaining on the reservations, heard their complaints about crooked agents and other bad treatment, and set things right. He decided he had to bring Geronimo and the others back from Mexico or face continuing raids and bloodshed. On the first of May of 1883, after much work setting up logistical supply for his troops in the field and persuading Mexican authorities to let him go after the Apaches in Mexico, Crook led 9 officers, 42 enlisted men (all mounted), 193 Apache scouts (on foot), and 5 pack trains of 266 mules with 76 civilian packers across the border into Mexico. It was one of the most daring military exercises ever conducted by the army and resulted in Crook, with little bloodshed, persuading the Apache chiefs and Geronimo to return to San Carlos. Most returned by mid-summer. However, Crook let Geronimo gather his people, and they did not begin to return until well into November of that year. Geronimo did not come in until February of 1884, driving a herd of stolen Mexican cattle he wanted the Apaches to develop for their own herds. The cattle were promptly confiscated, sold, and the money returned to the Mexican government for distribution back to the original owners. Needless to say, Geronimo was not happy about the government taking "his" cattle, but he accepted it. Given the opportunity to choose where they lived by General Crook, the returnees from the Sierra Madre chose to camp in the mountains on Turkey Creek in the summers and move down to within a few miles of Fort Apache in the winters. Lieutenant Britton Davis was put in charge of them to distribute supplies and to maintain order. The Apaches liked Davis. He was honest and fair and treated them as individuals.

Geronimo's Third and Last Breakout from San Carlos, 1885

FOR TWO YEARS THERE WERE NO APACHE RAIDS OR ATTACKS OF ANY KIND AFTER THE Apaches returned from the Sierra Madre in 1883, but trouble was developing. General Crook, since forcing the Apaches to the reservations in the mid-to-late 1870s, had ruled, among other things, that the Apaches could not make *tiswin* and the men could not abuse their wives. Lieutenant Davis tried to enforce these rules soon after Geronimo had returned from the Sierra Madre. When Davis first had a meeting with the chiefs to

After his third breakout from San Carlos in 1885, Geronimo discusses his surrender with General Crook, March 1886, in this C. S. Fly photograph.
PHOTO COURTESY OF LIBRARY OF CONGRESS

explain the rules, they were outraged, saying they had agreed to come back to the reservation and live peaceably, but didn't agree to Crook setting rules about how they lived and managed their family and social lives. They eventually stormed out of the meeting without agreeing to anything.

A year passed. The Apaches passed the winter at their camp near Fort Apache and then returned to Turkey Creek, where they were taught how to use farming tools (plows, etc.) to work their patches of crops. This went well, but while the Apaches trained with plows, the War Department and the Office of Indian Affairs became entangled in a bureaucratic struggle over who was in charge. This didn't directly affect the Apaches on Turkey Creek, but they became uneasy, worried that General Crook might be ordered away and the crooked agents would return. About this time, a young woman came to Davis with an arm broken in two places, her hair matted with blood, and a mass of welts and bruises on her shoulders. Davis had the post surgeon patch her up and put her husband in jail for two weeks. Several leaders demanded his release. Davis refused. Next, he arrested a man responsible for a *tiswin* drunk. Chihuahua and Mangas protested the arrest, but Davis wouldn't relent. The chiefs held a council and decided they would all get drunk on *tiswin*.

Early in the morning on Friday, May 15, 1885, the chiefs gathered with about thirty of their followers in front of Davis's tent. Davis's scouts gathered around to protect him. The tension in the air was electric. The Apaches were armed, and no women or children were in sight. Loco quietly presented their case until Chihuahua, who was clearly drunk, jumped up and reiterated their original arguments for making *tiswin*. When Davis again tried to explain the rules and got to wife beating, Nana stood and, before walking out, said to the translator, Mickey Free, "Tell the Nantan [Davis] that he can't advise me how to treat women. He's only a boy. I killed men before he was born." With Nana gone, Chihuahua continued his rant and said in so many words, "We all got drunk last night. What are you going to do about it? You can't put us all in jail." Davis said this was too serious for him to decide, that he would wire Crook, and let them know the answer.

Through a series of unfortunate circumstances, General Crook never saw Davis's wire and had no opportunity to resolve an issue over *tiswin*, drinking, and wife beating that led to Geronimo's last breakout from San Carlos. Thinking Crook was coming to fight them or put them in the guardhouse, Geronimo, Chihuahua, Naiche, Mangas, and Nana, along with 35 men, 8 boys old enough to use weapons, and 101 women and children, left the reservation and headed for Mexico on May 17, 1885. Three quarters of the band (about 400 men, women, and children) stayed on the reservation under Loco, Bonito, Gil-lee, and Chato. The Apaches who stayed on the reservation later told Crook and Davis that Geronimo and Mangas tricked the others into leaving by telling them they had killed Davis and Chato, and troops were coming to arrest the whole band and send them away.

By early November, with Geronimo operating out of Mexico, General Crook and his officers had troops all over the southwest on ready-to-march alert. Lieutenant Gen. Phillip

H. Sheridan, Commander in Chief of the Army, came from Washington to meet with General Crook at Fort Bowie. They decided to make a major effort to attack the Apache base in Mexico. The commands of Captains Wirt Davis and Crawford were reorganized and outfitted for the invasion. Captain Crawford crossed the border with his command on November 29, 1885. On January 9, 1886, Crawford's forward scouts found the Apache camp. After a hard night's march that left the supply pack train behind, the scouts had nearly surrounded the camp when braying burros gave them away.

The Chiricahuas disappeared in the early dawn gloom, leaving their supplies behind. Later that day, an Apache woman appeared and asked Crawford for a meeting with the chiefs the next day, and he agreed. Early the next morning, Mexican irregulars, thinking the scouts were hostiles, "mistakenly" shot Crawford in the head while he was waving a white flag and slightly wounded Tom Horn, his chief of scouts. The enraged scouts returned fire, killing all the Mexican officers and wounding five men. After withdrawing to a safe location and reconnecting with the supply train, Crawford died.

Second in command, Lt. Marion P. Maus, met with Naiche, Geronimo, and the other chiefs to discuss possible terms of surrender (the army still had many of their family members and had found and invaded their stronghold in Mexico, leading Geronimo to conclude there was no place to hide). Geronimo designated nine hostages to return with Maus to ensure his promise that he would meet with Crook near the border in "two moons to discuss surrender."

Maus returned to Fort Bowie, where the hostages were kept under guard. On February 5, 1886, Maus established a camp in Sonora about ten miles south of the Arizona border and waited for the Apaches to appear. On March 15, right on time, they signaled their approach and were all there by March 19, but Maus couldn't get them to cross the border. Instead, they chose a strong defensive position in a lava bed on top of a conical hill with deep ravines on the sides, and Maus made his camp half a mile away. Then he sent for General Crook, with whom Geronimo was anxious to talk. The meeting was held the afternoon of March 25. Geronimo gave his side first, saying he had believed there had been an official plot on his life (which was the gossip he had heard at San Carlos). When he finished, Crook looked him in the eye and said he was lying. Geronimo had promised to live in peace on the reservation, but had broken his word and had left to kill innocent people on both sides of the border. Therefore, his word was not to be trusted. An argument followed with charges and recriminations between the two.

The Chiricahuas returned to their camp and spent the next day debating what to do. Messages were sent back and forth between them, the Apaches trying to haggle their best terms. General Crook, who had been instructed by Sheridan to insist on unconditional surrender, believed he had been given some latitude on the final terms. Crook stipulated that all warriors (with the exception of old Nana) would be imprisoned in the East for a time not to exceed two years with such members of their families who wanted to stay with them. (He probably had Fort Marion [St. Augustine, Florida] in mind, which was where he had sent seventy-two plains warriors eleven years earlier, who returned to their people willing to keep the peace.)

The chiefs agonized over the deal until March 27. Chihuahua was the first to accept the terms, Geronimo, the last, when he and Crook finally shook hands. Crook told the Chiricahuas he would return to Fort Bowie the next day, and they could follow with Maus and the scouts. Crook set out early on March 28 to telegraph the news to General Sheridan.

Geronimo's Final Surrender and the Law of Unintended Consequences

AFTER HIS SURRENDER, GERONIMO MADE AN ERROR IN JUDGMENT THAT LED TO ALL the Chiricahuas being unjustly taken as prisoners of war, even if they were scouts still enrolled in the army who had helped track down Geronimo or if they had lived peaceably at San Carlos since their return from Mexico in 1883.

The night after their surrender, a bootlegger named Tribolett, who operated just south of the border and may have been in the pay of Tucson merchants known as the "Indian ring," making large profits off the Indian wars, provided the Chiricahuas whiskey that led

Apache prisoners of war at Fort Bowie awaiting shipment to Florida, 1886
PHOTO COURTESY OF NATIONAL ARCHIVES

to a major drunk. Tribolett, who had done business with Geronimo and was trusted, convinced him that there were plans to hang him as soon as he crossed the border. The next morning, after the Apaches had sobered up enough to ride, they went a short distance and camped scattered about in small groups. During that night, March 28, there was heavy drinking again. The next morning, Maus learned that Geronimo and Naiche with twenty men, fourteen women, and six children had slipped away, taking two horses and a mule from the herd. According to Maus, not a remaining soul knew when they left or where they were going. Eight of the twenty warriors were in their teens or early twenties and were related to Geronimo or Naiche.

Maus sent an officer and some of his scouts back to Fort Bowie with the remainder of the Chiricahuas. With his remaining scouts, Maus trailed the breakaways into the Sierra Madre but after a day had not caught sight of them. Two warriors who had left with the breakaways came in the next day. They said they had heard people leaving in the night and thought something had gone wrong. When they learned the truth, they returned. Back at the reservation, about four hundred Chiricahuas, including army scouts, had stayed true to their word since their return from Mexico in 1883 and were peacefully going about their business.

The same day Geronimo, his followers, and family left the main group, Crook arrived back at Fort Bowie and telegraphed General Sheridan, telling of the Chiricahua surrender and his terms. The next day, March 30, Sheridan, citing orders from President Cleveland, rejected Crook's conditions and ordered him to enter into negotiations for unconditional surrender, sparing only their lives, and to complete their destruction to prevent their escape unless they agreed to those terms. Such instructions were impossible to follow. Sheridan was too far away to understand the situation, and, for the first time, Crook, thinking the Apaches would scatter to the mountains when they heard Sheridan's terms, decided not to be, as he usually was, aboveboard in dealing with them. Later that day, a courier from Lieutenant Maus reported that Geronimo and Naiche had broken away from the main group. Crook wired Sheridan the bad news. Sheridan angrily shot back that it was Crook's fault that they had gotten away, that he should have had them under armed guard all the way.

Crook tried to explain what happened and why, but Sheridan wouldn't listen. Crook asked to be relieved of his command. Two days later, Sheridan ordered him to take over command of the Department of the Platte and appointed Brig. Gen. Nelson Appleton Miles to take over Crook's command in Arizona. The next day, he ordered Crook to ship the returning Chiricahuas to Fort Marion in St. Augustine, Florida, under the orders he had given him for their surrender two days earlier. There were seventy-seven in all—fifteen men, thirty-three women, and twenty-nine children, including two wives and three children of Geronimo, and two wives, two children, the mother, and other relatives of Naiche. They were delivered to Fort Marion on April 13.

General Miles relieved Crook on April 12. He was an experienced Indian fighter (the Lakota called him "Bear Coat Miles"), and he didn't hesitate in self-aggrandizement. Miles lacked Crook's quiet dedication, integrity, and understanding of the Apaches. He was anxious to show Sheridan how much better a general he was than Crook. Whatever Crook was for, Miles was against. Crook had told the army he could not use more than three thousand regular soldiers to advantage. Miles asked for five thousand soldiers (roughly a quarter of the army's strength) to capture Geronimo. He fired all but a few scouts he used for trackers, and took up the chase.

Miles soon discovered his horses couldn't climb the mountains and his soldiers didn't have the strength and stamina, common even with Apache women and children, to handle the rugged terrain on foot. Geronimo first struck in Sonora, and then on April 27, he entered the United States and raided at will even around San Carlos and Fort Apache. Despite the fact that he was only chasing eighteen warriors, fourteen women, and six children with a quarter of the U.S. Army, Miles didn't kill or capture a single Chiricahua.

Miles decided to turn his attention to Chiricahuas he could catch, the four hundred who were living peaceably on the reservation farming, cutting hay to sell at the post, raising livestock, and serving as scouts. The citizens of Arizona, who thought all Apaches were the same, hated them, and other tribes on the reservation disliked them for their arrogance as superior warriors and for causing trouble resulting from their breakouts. On July 3, Miles suggested to Sheridan that they be sent elsewhere. It was an idea the bureaucracies of the War Department and Department of Interior, rarely agreeing on anything, had frequently advocated, but no one had any idea where to send them. Crook had objected to their removal, and Sheridan had agreed with him, recalling the disaster when Victorio's people were uprooted by Clum from their Warm Springs reservation and marched to San Carlos. Now with Miles recommending it, Sheridan agreed, and it suddenly became official policy.

Given the money he was burning through using a quarter of the U.S. Army to chase Geronimo, Miles needed to show some success, and the peaceful Chiricahuas were it. He wanted to move them to a place near the Wichita Mountains in close proximity to Fort Sill on reservation land owned by the Kiowa, Kiowa-Apaches, and Comanche. Miles in his superb ignorance of Apaches didn't know these tribes were longtime enemies of the southwest Apaches and had they been forced to take the Chiricahuas on their lands, blood would have surely flowed. Furthermore, white settlers, primarily in Kansas, wanted Indian Nations land opened to white settlement and therefore opposed any addition to the Indian population there. Also, in 1887, Congress passed a law (the Dawes Act) prohibiting the settlement of Apaches and other Indians from New Mexico and Arizona in the Indian Nations.

After Geronimo surrendered in September 1886, the army and politicians were like dogs catching a car they were chasing; they didn't know what to do after they caught him. General Miles had disobeyed orders and lied at least twice to President Cleveland. (Miles denied he had offered two years in Florida and a well-stocked reservation with protection and reunion with their families. However, Geronimo and Naiche separately confirmed that was what Miles had promised.) Miles directed they be taken by train to the first available fort in Florida. The trains carrying the Apaches stopped at San Antonio, where the Apaches were kept at Fort Sam Houston for about six weeks while the War Department attempted to sort through the confusion created by Miles's lies. The Apaches believed they were about to be executed. Finally, at the direction of the president, all the Chiricahuas were shipped to Florida in late 1886. The men were sent to Fort Pickens on Santa Rosa Island in Pensacola Bay; the women and children, to Fort Marion at St. Augustine, Florida. Fort Marion was already overcrowded with seventeen scouts and Chihuahua's band when the new prisoners arrived. The army bureaucracy failed to get warm clothing and sufficient food to the half-naked Apaches their first winter in Florida, leaving them to suffer from exposure and disease and nearly starving.

Many died from tuberculosis and malaria, and General Crook applied enough pressure through newspapers discussing the injustice in imprisoning the Chiricahua scouts that the decision was made in 1887 to reunite the families at Fort Pickens and then move them to Mount Vernon Barracks, Alabama, about thirty miles north of Mobile. Mount Vernon Barracks was not suitable for the Apaches, either. There was nothing for them to do, as the soil was too sandy to farm, and the malaria and tuberculosis were as bad as in Florida.

A new search began in the East for reservation land. Reservation sites that were considered included twelve thousand acres on the Cherokee Reservation in North Carolina and several sites in the Tidewater area of Virginia, but all were too small for the prisoners to sustain themselves. In 1890, Secretary of War Proctor decided the best place to imprison the Chiricahuas was in the Indian Territory in Oklahoma. Proctor got around the Dawes Act prohibiting Arizona and New Mexico Indians from living in Indian Territory by announcing the Apaches would be kept at Fort Sill until Congress could make them a final reservation. There was a howl of Anglo outrage about carrying dangerous Apaches back to the West, but in October 1894, after much political infighting and maneuvering about what was best for the Apaches and safest for the Anglos, the Apaches were shipped to Fort Sill. There they built homes, farmed, and raised cattle. In 1913, four years after Geronimo had passed away, the Apache confinement ended, and 127 adults chose to return to New Mexico and live on the Mescalero Reservation. Eighty-seven adults chose to keep their places in Oklahoma.

Had Geronimo surrendered as he had told Crook he would, Crook would never have been forced to resign, and Miles would not have been a commander recommending relocation of the peaceful Chiricahuas, which Crook strongly opposed. Geronimo, in breaking away, had unintentionally sentenced four hundred of his people to twenty-seven years of prisoner of war internment.

APACHE SCOUTS

The Apache scouts are often assumed traitors to their people. As with so many other generalizations, that viewpoint is far too narrow to characterize these warriors accurately. When individual scouts are closely examined, we find heroes, outlaws, and survivors.

On June 4, 1871, Gen. George Crook assumed command of the U.S. Army's Department of Arizona. Arguably the best Indian fighter in the country, General Crook arrived in Tucson convinced that to effectively fight the Apaches, he had to have help from men who understood the desert and the Apaches, could survive in hard, unforgiving country, could follow a trail over ground where there were no tracks, and were willing to fight an enemy with no quarter given and none expected. Within a month, he was on his mule leading his soldiers on a 675-mile "practice" march from Tucson to Fort Bowie and around the Tonto Basin, during which officers and men got acquainted with one another and the countryside where they were to fight. This march included his first detachment of scouts, who Crook's Executive Officer, Lieutenant Bourke, said were a collection of "Navajos, Apaches, Opatas, Yaquis, Pueblos, Mexicans, Americans, and half-breeds of any tribe one could name." General Crook tried different combinations of tribes and men in his scout companies, but he consistently found that his best scouts were Apaches. It didn't take long for the mantra, "It takes an Apache to catch an Apache," to be identified as Crook's strategy.

Apache Scouts: Heroes, Outlaws, and Survivors

GENERAL CROOK ORGANIZED FIVE COMPANIES OF SCOUTS, EACH WITH BETWEEN THIRTY and thirty-six men and officers and each supporting an Arizona fort: Fort Apache, Fort Bowie, Fort Thomas, Camp Huachuca, and Fort Grant. A scout drew the same pay as regular troopers, earned rank, had three meals a day, slept in barracks, stood in formation, and learned to drill, and the army provided him a rifle, ammunition, and a few other supplies, including a uniform with a dress-wool military jacket (which they rarely wore). A scout could sign up for six months to a year, but he also could reenlist as many times as he wanted when his enlistment ended. When the scouts weren't on field assignment, they served as tribal policemen on the reservations associated with their forts.

Apache scouts at Fort Apache, Arizona, ca. 1880. The scout on the far right is the Apache Kid.
PHOTO COURTESY OF NATIONAL ARCHIVES

To understand why an Apache would be willing to soldier against his own people, it's important to realize that from the time Apaches were off their *tsachs* (cradleboards) they were taught to look after and defend themselves and to value independence above nearly everything else. The land of the Apaches couldn't support large groups of people. Therefore, an Apache had to know how to survive on his own, and he was taught to do what was best for himself and his family. An Apache warrior followed leaders with whom he was usually related by blood or who were so good at raiding and warfare that it was to his advantage to follow that leader. However, when the leader went to war or on a raid (war was usually for revenge killing, raiding for supplies), the follower was not obliged to go, unless he gave his word that he would, and if the leader had two or three unsuccessful raids or too many warriors were killed in his wars and raids, he soon didn't have anyone to lead.

For Apache men on reservations with little to do except maybe farm (women's work) or sit around and talk or occasionally hunt, the opportunity to earn money fighting, even if the combatants were their own people, and to be given all the soldier accouterments, including a rifle and bullets, was irresistible; and, true to the custom of keeping his word to his leader, when an Apache made his mark on a paper for an enlistment term, he kept the agreement. Many Apache men who were good warriors were scouts for the army at one time or another, and within the ranks of those scouts were heroes, outlaws, and survivors.

A clear picture of an Apache scout's ability and courage and that some were unquestionably heroes is shown by the fact that at Fort Apache, on April 12, 1875, General Crook personally presented the Congressional Medal of Honor to ten Apache scouts for their service in the 1872–1873 Winter Campaign in Arizona against the western Apaches.

Six years after General Crook awarded the Medals of Honor to his Apache scouts, Geronimo, Naiche, Juh, and other well-known leaders led a breakout of seventy-four warriors and their families from the San Carlos Reservation and, seven months later, returned to force the respected Mimbreño leader Loco and his followers to join them in the Sierra Madre. In May 1883, General Crook led 193 Apache scouts, 50 troopers, and 5 pack trains of mules carrying supplies on one of the most daring and successful military exercises ever conducted by the U.S. Army. The scouts were on foot and ran over four hundred miles during the expedition with only their weapons in hand. They raced far ahead of the mounted troopers and pack trains down river valleys and over mountains in some of the most rugged country on earth. Reaching the end-of-the-day camp locations early, they took time to hunt and keep the expedition supplied with fresh meat.

A Mimbreño (originally a White Mountain, but Mimbreño by marriage), Tzoe, also known to the troopers as Peaches because of his smooth, fair skin, had lived in the Apache Sierra Madre camps, and he guided the campaign to them in Mexico. Without Tzoe, it's likely General Crook never would have found the Apaches in Mexico, preventing much bloodshed on both sides of the border by Americans, Mexicans, and Apaches.

When Geronimo left San Carlos the third time and refused to come in after giving his word to General Crook that he would, more than half the Chiricahua and Mimbreño warriors who had stayed on the reservation offered their services as scouts to bring him in. It was Kayitah and Martine, scouts in Lieutenant Gatewood's company, who talked Geronimo into surrendering in March 1886.

Massai was one of the Chiricahua scouts who had stayed on the reservation with his wife and two daughters when Geronimo broke out of the reservation the third time. After Geronimo surrendered in early September 1886, the army swept up all the Chiricahuas, including the scouts who had helped to find Geronimo, and shipped them to Florida as prisoners of war. Massai and his friend, a Tonkawa, Gray Lizard, were the only ones to escape from the train to Florida. Massai, leaving a wife and two daughters on the train, and Gray Lizard walked at least six hundred miles back to the Capitan Mountains. Gray Lizard left Massai near Sierra Blanca and went on to Mescal Mountain, near Globe, Arizona, and was never seen again. Massai hid out on the great sacred mountain, Sierra Blanca, stole a young Mescalero woman for a new wife, and, hiding with his wife, had six children while being accused of numerous thefts and killings. During that time, it is reported that Massai often rode with another scout who was being hunted, Apache Kid.

At one time, Al Sieber, Chief of Scouts, considered Kid his best scout, but Kid made a major life error in a revenge killing for his father's murder. In 1887, Kid was accused (he was actually innocent) of shooting Al Sieber in the ankle during a near riot when surrendering for the revenge killing. After a court-martial sentenced him to death by firing squad, General Miles commuted the sentence, saying it was unjustified and too harsh. The court then sent Kid to a life sentence on Alcatraz Island, but that sentence was also overturned, and he was freed to return to San Carlos.

The Territory of Arizona again arrested Kid in 1889 for shooting Al Sieber, using a Supreme Court ruling on a technicality about the authority of territorial judges. After that trial, he was sentenced to seven years hard labor in the Yuma Territorial Prison. While on the way to prison, he and other Apache prisoners killed the sheriff and his deputy accompanying them and escaped. Many tales have been told about Apache Kid's fate after the escape, but few if any have been verified. He was supposedly killed several times by posses, but a man who knew him personally swears he saw Kid in Mexico in 1924.

In one of the most shameful episodes in American history, the Chiricahua scouts who had served the army long and honorably and had lived peacefully for years on the Arizona reservations were made prisoners of war and shipped east with the Geronimo renegades to languish in captivity for the next twenty-seven years.

Most of the scouts were still respected by their brothers after they were taken as prisoners of war, but one, Chato, was not. Lieutenant Britton Davis claimed that Chato was one of the finest men of any race he had known, and General Crook boasted of his scout's effectiveness and loyalty. However, the Apaches viewed him as being hungry for power and wanting more control as a leader than they were willing to cede. Hence, when the Chiricahuas were released as prisoners of war and returned to Mescalero, Chato was shunned. He chose to live by himself on the summit of Apache Pass about ten miles from the Mescalero agency, while the rest of the Chiricahuas moved to White Tail, about twenty miles from the agency. There was no water at the place where Chato decided to live and he had to haul a weekly supply in barrels he filled at the agency. In 1934 Chato died from injuries suffered in an automobile accident. He was ninety-three years old.

Scout Bigmouth, the last living Apache scout from the Apache wars, died when he was about 103 years old, at Mescalero, New Mexico, on November 28, 1958. He didn't speak English, but through the translations of his stories by his devoted eldest son, Percy, who as Eve Ball said was one of the best-known and beloved individuals on the reservation, he gave to the historians the Apache view of one who had lived through the hellhole days of Bosque Redondo as a young boy, through the early reservation days as a young man, and as a tribal policeman and army scout in his mature manhood. Percy, who as a young boy had a spinal injury and never married, took care of Scout Bigmouth in his elderly years, and he passed away from a heart attack at age sixty-eight on January 5, 1959, just a few weeks after Scout Bigmouth. Percy provided the translation of what his father said during Eve Ball interviews and, fearing the loss of the Mescalero culture, later filled Big Chief writing tablets with its stories and history he had learned through all the years listening to his father.

Al Sieber, Chief of Scouts

AL SIEBER IS ONE OF THE TRUE, BUT LITTLE-KNOWN, LARGER-THAN-LIFE CHARACTERS who helped the army conquer the Apaches with Apaches. He was among the best leaders of these scouts, and within a year of his employment, he became one of General Crook's most trusted guides.

The Apaches knew Al Sieber was an expert rifle shot and a prankster. He was physically tough, and when he gave his word, he kept it. Dan Thrapp, Sieber's biographer, says that most of the punitive expeditions he went on were successful; those from which he

Al Sieber rode with his Apache scouts in much the same way Herman W. Hansen illustrated in his painting *The Scout*, ca. 1900.

was absent met with few triumphs. When asked to explain his ability to control the fiercest Apaches and to use them effectively against renegades, Sieber said, "I do not deceive them, but always tell them the truth. When I tell them I'm going to kill them, I do it, and when I tell them I am their friend, they know it." Thrapp claims that Sieber was involved in more Indian fights than Daniel Boone, Jim Bridger, and Kit Carson combined. He was as good at tracking as most Apaches. The story goes that at the San Carlos Reservation, an Apache strongly considered leaving but decided against it, no matter how miserable life might become, because he said Sieber would find him even if he left no tracks.[1]

Al Sieber served twenty years in the scouts from 1872 to 1892. During that time, he was involved in many of the more famous campaigns and battles against the Apaches, including the 1872–1873 winter campaign in the Tonto Basin and the battle of Big Dry Wash, and he was chief of scouts during General Crook's Sierra Madre Campaign in 1883, which returned an estimated seven hundred Apaches hiding in and raiding from the Sierra Madre to San Carlos with relatively little bloodshed. At San Carlos Sieber continued as chief of scouts. Two years later he made the mistake of his career and misevaluated the importance of Lt. Britton Davis's telegram to General Crook requesting a judgment about the Chiricahuas making *tiswin*. Davis was requesting help in a serious matter involving discipline of Chiricahua leaders, but Sieber judged it was just about a *tiswin* drunk and Crook never saw Davis's message. Crook not responding to the telegram led the Chiricahuas to believe he was coming to attack them and, led by Naiche, Chihuahua, Mangas, and Geronimo, thirty warriors jumped the reservation in May of 1885 to start another Geronimo war.

Sieber retired from the army after being crippled during gunfire when his best scout, Apache Kid, was to be disciplined. After retiring from the army, Sieber supervised Apache ground crews building a road from the Roosevelt Dam site north along Tonto Creek. On February 17, 1907, Sieber's crew had been attempting to move a five- or six-ton round boulder out of the way for nearly two days. It wouldn't budge. Sieber crawled under it to determine the problem, and it fell on him immediately, crushing him to death. It is said that Apaches all over Arizona grieved when they heard the news.

Apache Scout Power

The oral history Eve Ball recorded about the Chiricahua scouts showed that some had Power (apparent supernatural gifts) that aided them as trackers. Asa Daklugie, youngest son of Juh and nephew of Geronimo, told Eve of the Power some scouts had to track across long stretches of trackless hard ground and bare stone. "Maybe a stone be moved and turned over. Maybe the grass or weeds be stepped on and broken off near the ground. But one doing it [tracking] could almost tell how long ago it was done. Just a few were experienced trailers, maybe three or four of the band. They go ahead and study the trail. Maybe a wild country and they try to find the trail. They find it in a few hours."

Eustace Fatty, grandson of Gordo, half brother to Daklugie and Charles Martine, said, "In soft places, I could trail, but in the rocks I could not, but some Indians could see it. I don't know how they do it. It was some kind of Power. But they did follow it on the run."

James Kaywaykla [his "grandfather" was Nana] told how some scouts had a much keener sense of smell than the Americans. "If the Mormons brought fruit—peaches, apples—we could smell that for a long distance, maybe several miles . . . A man left Fort Apache, and Asa told that he and Mangas [son of Mangas Coloradas] and [their] party are out with him and this man came to him. This man told the Indians that when he went to their camp he could smell them, that he followed the scent like a wild animal does . . . He was a Warm Springs [Mimbreño]."

Some Apache scouts seemed to have supernatural power to follow trails that seemed otherwise impossible to follow, as Herman Hansen illustrated in his painting *Apache on the Trail*, ca. 1900.

Apache Scouts and the Salt River Cave Fight

THE APACHE SCOUTS WERE INVALUABLE TO THE ARMY WHEN GENERAL CROOK BEGAN his first campaign against the western Apaches. General Crook's 1872–1873 Winter Campaign was fought mainly in the Tonto Basin. Two Tonto Apaches, Delshay and Chunz, had been leading raids that had killed more than forty farmers and ranchers and taken numerous cattle and horses. Scouts finally located Delshay and a large number of his warriors hiding in a shallow cave on a shelf halfway up a thousand-foot-high cliff on the Salt River in the Tonto Basin. With their officers, Captain Taylor and Lieutenant Bourke, they climbed down the cliff to the Salt River during the freezing cold night of December 27, 1872, and deployed around the cave, hiding behind rocks and trees until daylight.

With the coming dawn, they called to the raiders and told them to surrender and come out. Because his defensive position was so strong, Delshay refused to surrender. A terrific firefight ensued, and seventy-six of Delshay's warriors were killed. A scout named Nantaje was able to lead the scouts to the mouth of the cave by firing in the opposite direction from which he moved and filling the cave with deadly ricochets. When all the scouts were in place, they rushed inside the cave but found little resistance. About thirty of Delshay's surviving warriors were wounded, and only a very few escaped. Sixteen months later, ten of the Apache scouts were awarded the Medal of Honor for their courage and bravery at the cave fight and other battles in that campaign. One of the scouts winning the Medal of Honor was Alchisaye, who Henry Farny painted in 1894.

Although the army's Apache scouts came from nearly all the Apache bands, Chiricahua scouts were instrumental in nearly all government operations to control the Apaches. They served General Crook in the Tonto Wars, helped keep the Mescaleros penned up in 1880 after the army invaded their reservation, fought in the Victorio and Nana Wars, and were the predominant force (193 Indians and 50 troopers) when Crook went into Mexico to bring Geronimo and the other Apaches back to San Carlos in 1883. They were instrumental in helping Lieutenant Gatewood find Geronimo and convince him to surrender in September of 1886.

Alchisaye was a famous Apache scout who was painted by Henry Farny, ca. 1894. Alchisaye won the Congressional Medal of Honor for his service as a scout during the Salt River Cave Fight in 1872.

PHOTO COURTESY OF SHARLOT HALL MUSEUM LIBRARY AND ARCHIVES, AL-CHE-SAY, 1500.0165.0000

Apache Scout Tzoe, "Peaches"

On September 25, 1881, after the army had tried to arrest, and in the ensuing melee killed the Apache prophet Noch-ay-del-klinne at Cibecue Creek on the San Carlos Reservation in Arizona, Naiche, Geronimo, Chato, Juh, and their followers left the reservation and ran for the Blue Mountains (Sierra Madre) in Sonora and Chihuahua, Mexico, raiding, looting, and murdering anyone in their path. Twenty-one-year-old White Mountain Apache Tzoe (Yellow Wolf or Coyote), married to two Mimbreño women related to Chato, had been forced to join them when they swept Loco's people off the reservation.

The Apaches believed they had a sanctuary in the Blue Mountains that protected them from the American army and allowed them to raid across the border at will, and that, even if the Americans came into Mexico, they would never find their camps on some of the most rugged terrain on earth. The Apaches were right. By the spring of 1883, after many schemes, attempts, and fights trying to stop the raids, General Crook was convinced he had to go into Mexico and force the Apaches to return to San Carlos. He knew he needed a guide to find the Apache camps in Mexico, but he was determined to go south whether he had one or not and began preparations in Willcox, Arizona.

In late March 1883, Chihuahua, Bonito, and Chato led a six-day raid into Arizona and New Mexico that covered over four hundred miles and killed twenty-six whites. Tzoe was on that raid. His two wives and a child had been killed in the battle of the Arroyo when Loco's people were forced to join Geronimo's people in the Sierra Madre.[1]

During Chato's raid, Tzoe lost his best friend, Beneactiney, in an attack on a charcoal burner's camp. He was so distraught that he told Chato and the other warriors that his Power said he had to return to San Carlos to help his people. The raiders gave him enough supplies to get to San Carlos, and they amiably parted company.

Lieutenant Britton Davis and his scouts captured Tzoe just outside the reservation boundary. After questioning him, Davis wired General Crook in Willcox that he believed Tzoe, called "Peaches" by the troopers because of his smooth, fair skin and good looks, might be his guide to the Apache camps. Crook sent for him and found Tzoe straightforward, honest, and willing to guide him to the Apache camps in Mexico. There was

This photograph of Tzoe, or Penaltishn, was taken in 1884 by Frank Randall.

PHOTO COURTESY OF NATIONAL ARCHIVES

concern that if scouts in the campaign with relatives in the Sierra Madre learned that Tzoe knew where the camps were, they would try to assassinate him. Crook made him a first sergeant so it appeared natural for him to be in the column lead, and other trusted scouts were appointed to watch his back.

With Tzoe leading the way for nearly two hundred scouts, fifty troopers, and five pack trains of mules, General Crook found the Apache camps and after long talks with their leaders convinced them to return to San Carlos. The five hundred to seven hundred Apaches put up little resistance when they were found. They were shocked and dismayed that they no longer had sanctuary in Mexico, that they could be found there at all, and that their own people worked for the army. As a result of his work on the expedition, Tzoe became one of General Crook's most trusted and able scouts.

Although he might appear to be a traitor to his people, Tzoe in fact saved many Apache, Mexican, and American lives by his service. He also served in 1916 as General "Black Jack" Pershing's personal scout in the hunt for Pancho Villa after his Columbus, New Mexico, raid. Tzoe died around 1933 at the age of seventy-three.

Chato: Survivor and Apache Judas?

CHATO, DESPITE BEING A PARIAH TO HIS PEOPLE, WAS A GOOD EXAMPLE OF THE SCOUTS who survived despite every adversity. Lieutenant Britton Davis claimed that Chato was one of the finest men of any race he had known, and General Crook boasted of his effectiveness and loyalty. There were a number of Chiricahua scouts who were imprisoned with Geronimo's people, but apparently only Chato was viewed as a traitor. The other scouts seemed to be accepted and treated the same as the rest of the band. Nana rejected Chato as his segundo (number two) before he became a scout. The Apache elders considered Chato rude and disrespectful.[1]

James Kaywaykla, a Warm Springs Apache who was a young boy with a near photographic memory for personalities, says in *Victorio, Recollections of a Warm Springs Apache,* that the White Eyes who killed Chato's brother and father had no more implacable enemy. In March of 1883, Chato and Bonito led a twenty-six-man, six-day raid (the Apaches called this Chihuahua's Raid) into southern Arizona and New Mexico—a lightning strike that covered 400 to 450 miles with the intent of taking horses and ammunition and killing any White Eye in their path. Chato only slept while riding on his horse. It was on this raid that Judge and Mrs. H. C. McComas were killed on their way to Lordsburg, and Charlie, their six-year-old son, was taken. (This is also the same raid in which Tzoe's best friend, Beneactiney, was killed.)

When Tzoe led the scouts into the Sierra Madre, Bonito's camp was the only one where shots were fired as the scouts took it over and killed several people. General Crook was careful to see that the survivors were treated well, and after long talks with the Apache chiefs and leading warriors, Chato among them, they agreed to peacefully return to San Carlos. General Crook made a strong impression on Chato. After returning to San Carlos, Chato decided to become a scout and was soon the first sergeant in Company B under the direction of Lt. Britton Davis. Davis was to write in 1929, "[Chato was] one of the finest men, red or white, I have ever known."

Chato served Lieutenant Davis well and saved him from Apache assassination at least once during the next three years, and he rode with Lieutenant Gatewood in 1886

1884 Frank Randall photograph of Chato, Mimbreño Apache scout

PHOTO COURTESY OF NATIONAL ARCHIVES

to convince Geronimo to surrender. After Geronimo surrendered to General Miles, Miles gave the order to make all Chiricahuas prisoners of war, regardless of whether they had been scouts or living in peace on the reservation, and ship them to Florida. Miles decided it would be politically prudent to send ten Chiricahua leaders, Chato heading the delegation, to Washington to negotiate their removal from their homeland. Chato appealed to Secretary of War William C. Endicott to leave the peaceful Chiricahuas and scouts in Arizona and asked for a "paper" that said as much. Endicott gave him a paper that said Chato had been in Washington and pinned a silver medal on his coat. The delegates all believed they had saved their homeland. Three months later, they were prisoners of war in Florida.

Geronimo and others blamed Chato for betraying the Chiricahuas to the White Eyes. Chato survived the twenty-seven-year prisoner of war internment in the East but was a bitter old man when he was released at Fort Sill, Oklahoma, in 1913 and returned to the New Mexico Mescalero Reservation. There the factional hatred that living together as prisoners of war had kept in check finally made him a pariah to the other Chiricahuas. Geronimo's nephew, Asa Daklugie, told Eve Ball in *Indeh*, "And Chato! I don't suppose that any White Eye but you will ever be convinced that Chato was not all he represented himself to be: the leader of Chihuahua's raid, and a faithful and loyal scout to Crook and Davis. If he were the latter, it was simply because nobody else could offer him more prestige. To the Apaches, he was the arch traitor—as James Kaywaykla said—a sort of Benedict Arnold to us."

Chato chose to live by himself on the summit of Apache Pass about ten miles from the Mescalero agency. He died from injuries suffered in an automobile accident in 1934 at age ninety-three.

The Apache Kid: Trials, Escape, Renegade

One of the most famous and fascinating outlaws to appear in the late-nineteenth-century Southwest was the former Apache scout Has-kay-bay-nay-ntayl ("Brave and tall and will come to a mysterious end"), also known as Apache Kid. After he escaped while being transported to Yuma Prison and avoided being caught in one of the greatest manhunts in Arizona history, Kid lived up to his Apache name because no one knows for certain how his life ended. The Kid's unjust court-martial, pardon, retrial, his famous escape, and the subsequent attempt to capture him and his fellow escapees culminated in the greatest manhunt in Arizona history.[1]

Trials of the Apache Kid

IN MAY 1887, AL SIEBER, CHIEF OF SCOUTS, AND CAPTAIN PIERCE OF THE SAN CARLOS agency went on an inspection tour to Fort Apache and the White River subagency. Kid, a sergeant of scouts and a Sieber favorite, was left in charge of the San Carlos scouts and guardhouse. The Apaches learned that Pierce and Sieber would be gone for a while and decided it was a good time for a major home-brew *tiswin* party. When Kid learned that his own band (registered as the "I" band by the military) was making tiswin, he sneaked away alone early one evening to join family and friends in a good drunk. From there Kid, two half brothers, and two other scouts went AWOL for five days to kill an Apache named Rip. Rip had encouraged his brother to kill Kid's father, Toga-de-chuz. When Sieber returned and learned he had five scouts AWOL and why they were gone, he sent word that Kid and the others were to report to him immediately. They came in about five o'clock in the afternoon on June 1, 1887, and went directly to Sieber's tent, where a big crowd of Indians had gathered to see what kind of punishment Sieber would deliver to his scouts, especially his favorite. Captain Pierce joined Sieber at his tent and ordered the scouts to put down their weapons. Kid was first to comply. Pierce pointed to the guardhouse and said, "Calaboose." From the crowd, Pierce saw a gun being leveled in his direction and that of Sieber. A shot rang out. There was a scuffle between Sieber and the scouts over the firearms they had just surrendered. Bullets filled the air, and Sieber was hit in the ankle with a .45-70 slug (then standard army ammunition) that crippled him for life. It was never proven who shot Sieber, but it definitely wasn't Kid or the others who had been AWOL. They were too busy escaping. After a long chase, lasting nearly a month, Kid and the others surrendered to General Miles on June 25, 1887.

All five scouts, including Kid, were court-martialed and sentenced to death by firing squad. General Miles, then Commander of the Department of Arizona, refused to accept the death sentence. The court reconvened and changed the death sentence to a life at hard labor at Fort Leavenworth, Kansas. Kid and the other scouts were held in the San Carlos guardhouse from June 25, 1887, until January 23, 1888, when Lt. Gen. Sheridan, Commanding General of the U.S. Army, ordered that, instead of Fort Leavenworth, they

Has-kay-bay-nay-ntayl (Apache Kid) before the Globe Trial of 1889
PHOTO COURTESY OF LYNDA SÁNCHEZ/EVE BALL COLLECTION

be imprisoned on Alcatraz Island in California. After reviewing the court-martial records, Judge Advocate General G. Norman Lieber found prejudice among officers serving on the jury, that the punishment didn't fit the crime, and that the interpreter, Antonio Diaz, had probably been out of line when the prisoners first surrendered to Sieber and Pierce, telling them they would go to Alcatraz for life. Secretary of War William C. Endicott agreed with Lieber's findings, and on October 29, 1888, remitted the sentences to time served and ordered the prisoners be allowed to return to San Carlos. They arrived back home on the stage from the train station at Casa Grande, Arizona, and upon crossing the Gila River at San Carlos, the Tenth Cavalry band met them and played for them along the way back into camp. Upon seeing this, friends of Al Sieber were infuriated. Three of the scouts were never heard from again. However, Kid and Bach-e-on-al would within a year again be facing an unjust jury trial.

Arizona Territory had a dual judicial system in which judges served as both federal and territorial judges. In criminal cases, a judge had to decide whether the procedures followed would be federal or territorial. If territorial, the guilty were sent to Yuma Territorial Prison. In March of 1885, an act of Congress required that an Indian committing murder whether on or off a reservation had to be tried according to territorial law in the same courts and manner as other persons within the exclusive jurisdiction of the United States. In 1888, in response to an appeal by the Indian Rights Association, the Supreme Court ruled that the Federal District Courts had usurped the power of the Arizona Territorial Courts in convicting Apaches of murder and ordered them freed. Simmering anger and frustration among the white community and the military over getting "justice" for Indian criminals became a roaring fire. The territory was determined to arrest and retry those Apaches and others freed by the Supreme Court decision. Since being shot in the ankle in June 1887, Al Sieber had two years to feel the pain of his wound that would never heal and to let his resentment toward those he held ultimately responsible grow.

By October 14, 1889, a stack of complaints for Indians to be rearrested and tried in Arizona Territorial Court was in the hands of Gila County Sheriff Glenn Reynolds. The Supreme Court decision that freed the Indians already in prisons had absolutely nothing to do with the Kid case. However, Case No. 157 in Sheriff Reynolds complaints, stated, ". . . the defendant (Kid) did on the first day of June 1887 assault with intent to murder one Al Sieber—warrant of arrest issued." Within several days, all the Indians except Kid had been arrested, and soon, through a clever ploy of pretending to be a cowboy by Reynolds's chief deputy, so was Kid. Kid, Say-es, and Pash-ten-tah (who told the court, for reasons unknown, his name was Bach-e-on-al) were all tried for attempted murder against Al Sieber. The accusations at the trial and what really happened made no sense. Kid and the two others accused of shooting Al Sieber proved they were already gone, trying to escape, when the shooting occurred. Even Sieber admitted as much, but still wanted to see them in jail. They were clearly innocent. Nevertheless, a jury found all three guilty. Kid, Say-es, and Pash-ten-tah were each sentenced to seven years at hard labor at the Yuma Territorial Prison. Later that afternoon, the prisoners were lined up in front of the courthouse for group pictures, probably taken by some enterprising newspaper reporter.

In the post-trial photograph, Kid with his felt hat and knotted scarf looks the neatest of the prisoners bound for Yuma. After all the betrayal he had endured, he was still abiding by American rules. His brass reservation tag can be clearly seen on his left breast coat pocket.

The Escape of the Apache Kid

THE APACHE KID AND SEVEN OTHER APACHES WERE SENTENCED TO YUMA TERRITORIAL Prison after a trial in Globe, Arizona. Sheriff Glenn Reynolds, who had served the warrants on the Apache prisoners, was required to transport them to the Yuma Territorial Prison. The weather was cold, with winter coming on, and Tom Horn, ex-scout and Indian fighter who sometimes worked as a deputy for Reynolds, had decided to attend a roping contest in Phoenix that weekend. Al Sieber offered to send a contingent of Apache scouts from San Carlos to accompany Reynolds, but Reynolds turned him down, saying, "I don't need your scouts, I can take those Indians alone with a corncob and a lightning bug." To replace Tom Horn, Reynolds hired William "Hunkydory" Holmes to help guard the prisoners. Holmes had written a poem, "Hunkydory" that earned him his nickname. He was a typical tough-nut frontiersman who liked his liquor and singing his poems in bars.

Sheriff Reynolds planned hauling the prisoners by stagecoach, a trip taking two days, to Casa Grande, where he could load them onto the train to Yuma. He hired the Middleton Stage Line, a company privately owned by Eugene Middleton, who had had a number of disastrous brushes with Apaches. At first Middleton was reluctant to take the job, but he finally agreed after Reynolds, his good friend, goaded him into going. Middleton used the coach Reynolds wanted—a new, heavy-duty, thoroughbrace Concord with three wide seats, two facing forward and one with its back to the driver. The eight prisoners wore handcuffs and leg irons and were chained together two-by-two at the wrists and ankles when off the stage. A ninth prisoner, Jesus Avott, a Mexican horse thief sentenced to a year at Yuma, was considered so inconsequential that he rode unshackled on the boot. Middleton, driving the coach, picked up the prisoners, Sheriff Reynolds, and Hunkydory Holmes early Friday on a cool, overcast morning at the Globe Jail, November 1, 1889. Hunkydory Holmes rode inside the coach and carried a Winchester and a pistol. Sheriff Reynolds rode his horse, Tex, and carried a double-barreled shotgun and a .45 Colt. Middleton was armed with a pistol.

The stage headed south from Globe to the 66 Ranch and stopped at the tollgate to pay for access to the Globe–Pinal Summit toll road. Sheriff Reynolds paid $7.00 for the

Photograph of convicted Apaches taken after the Globe Trial of October 1889. The prisoners are, left to right and beginning with the top row: El-cahn, Hos-cal-te, Say-es, Apache Kid, Bob McIntosh; bottom row left to right: Has-ten-tu-du-jay, Nah-deiz-az, Bach-e-on-al, Bi-the-ja-be-tish-to-ce-an, and Hale. Bob McIntosh was later found innocent and Nah-deiz-az was hanged. Note names on photo are inconsistent with Arizona Historical Society records.

PHOTO COURTESY OF SHARLOT HALL MUSEUM LIBRARY AND ARCHIVES AL-CHE-SAY

stage and horses and twelve people. From there, it was a long, slow haul to the summit at Pioneer Pass, where the prisoners were off-loaded to eat their midday meal. Horses were changed and the coach axles greased. They headed for Riverside Station, forty miles south of Globe. Hunkydory Holmes serenaded the sullen Apaches with his singing, and Sheriff Reynolds took occasional practice shots at prickly pear cactus with his revolver. Down the last seven-mile grade to the Gila River, a drizzling rain turned into a downpour, making them hurry to get across before the river rose.

At Riverside Station, the Apaches, Jesus Avott, and their guards had a good meal of Irish stew, rice pudding, bread, and coffee. The Apaches were chained together and slept sitting up on a bench facing their guard. Jesus Avott was allowed to sit alone in a chair without handcuffs. Reynolds and Hunkydory took turns watching the prisoners through the night while occasionally visiting the station's well-stocked bar. Middleton roused everyone at 4:00 a.m. with the intention of leaving at five o'clock in order to make the 4:00 p.m. train connection at Casa Grande. He was concerned about the upcoming steep Kelvin Grade they would have to climb four miles southeast of Riverside Station. The prisoners would have to get out and walk in order for the horses to pull the stage up the steep grade, which, with the trail wet, would make it an even harder pull. After the prisoners were loaded on the stage, Reynolds made a fatal mistake and decided to leave his horse at the station. Two Apaches rode on top with Middleton and Reynolds, and Holmes rode inside on the first seat with the other six Apaches on the two facing seats and Jesus Avott again outside on the boot.

The stage reached Kelvin Grade in the foggy dawn and stopped to unload all the prisoners, except Kid and Hos-cal-te, who were considered too dangerous to be allowed out. Middleton drove the stage up the incline and slowly pulled away from the straggling prisoners led by Reynolds, who, since it was cold and wet, wore gloves, had his heavy overcoat buttoned over his holstered pistol, and carried his shotgun in the crook of his arm. He was followed by the prisoners handcuffed in pairs: Sayes to El-cahn, Has-ten-tu-du-jay to Bi-the-ja-be-tish-to-ce-an, and Bach-e-on-al to Hale. Hunkydory Holmes brought up the rear carrying his rifle. Jesus Avott walked alone close by the sheriff.

As the stage slowly pulled out of sight, Sayes and El-cahn, edging up close to Reynolds, saw their chance and pounced. They held Reynolds between them and grappled for his shotgun. At the same time, Bach-e-on-al and Hale turned on Hunkydory Holmes, knocked him to the ground, and Bach-e-on-al, grabbing his rifle, shot Holmes, killing him instantly. He turned the rifle on Reynolds, who couldn't get to the pistol buttoned under his coat, and killed him. Jesus Avott decided that if he tried to interfere, the law would think he was in on the break. He ran up the hill to warn Middleton.

Middleton, hearing shots, didn't think anything of it because Reynolds had been target practicing all the day before. When he heard Avott shouting the Apaches had killed Reynolds and Holmes, he told him to get in the stage, but Avott saw Bach-e-on-al coming up the road with Holmes's rifle and headed for the bushes instead. The next thing Middleton knew, Bach-e-on-al was beside the stage aiming for him with Holmes's rifle. Middleton ducked and the bullet hit him in the mouth, barely missing his teeth and spine and rendering him temporarily paralyzed. He fell to the ground but didn't lose consciousness. In a pool of blood, he realized the Apaches, who had stripped all the valuables off Reynolds and Holmes, had gathered around the coach and were setting Hos-cal-te and Kid free. Then they surrounded him and took all his possessions while El-cahn raised a rock over his head, but Kid grabbed his arm. The Apaches had an angry discussion before El-cahn tossed the rock and Middleton's life was saved. They took everything of value and disappeared into the wilderness. Before the end of the day, the greatest manhunt in Arizona history was underway.

Apache Kid, Renegade

AFTER THE APACHE KID AND THE OTHER PRISONERS ESCAPED INTO THE WILDERNESS, Eugene Middleton's paralysis from being shot in the mouth soon passed, and he staggered to his feet. He realized he was too weak to crawl back up on the stage or even to handle the team, and so he decided to walk back to Riverside Station. Crawling, stumbling, fighting nausea, he found the bodies of Reynolds and Holmes and wobbled on to Riverside Station, a little more than four miles away.

The stage was just leaving for Globe when the passengers saw a staggering man coming up the road. They agreed to take care of Middleton, while the stage driver, Shorty Sayler, decided the fastest way to get to Globe to spread the alarm was to take Reynolds's horse. He changed horses at the station in Pioneer and made the forty-mile trip in record time, getting to Globe at noon. The telegrapher at San Carlos took the news to Al Sieber, who was in bed still recovering from his ankle wound incurred sixteen-plus months earlier. Sieber said, "I was afraid of that, and that was my reason for offering the scout escort to Casa Grande." He ordered a twenty-man scout detail from San Carlos under Lieutenant Watson to pick up the trail.

Jesus Avott, the Mexican horse thief, hid in the brush until the Apaches disappeared, returned to the stage, found only blood where Middleton's body had been, and cut one of the team horses loose from the stage to ride to Florence, the next town, about twenty-five miles away, for help. The horse promptly threw him off.

A horse wrangler for the Zellewager Ranch, Andronico Lorona, seeing the stopped stagecoach, drove his twelve horses over for a look, found Avott, heard his story about the eight Apache convicts headed for Yuma escaping, took a gentle horse from his remuda, and sent Avott on to Florence. Lorona carried the word back to his foreman, who then sent a few cowboys back to the stage to guard the bodies of Reynolds and Holmes until help arrived.

In Globe, Deputy Sheriff Ryan (the same man who had tricked and arrested Kid for the trial) received a telegram from Sheriff Fryer in Florence (since the killings had

As a renegade, Kid was accused of many ambushes, murders, and thefts, but actual evidence was nonexistent or lacking. Henry Farny painted *An Apache Ambush* in 1892, which is indicative of Kid's modus operandi after escaping on his way to Yuma Prison.

occurred in his county, Fryer would be in charge of the investigation) that a posse and a coroner's jury were on their way to the Riverside Station and the scene of the crime.

For his effort, Avott was pardoned and didn't have to serve any prison time. Although Kid killed no one during the Kelvin Grade escape, he was now legally culpable and would be hunted like the others as posses, cowboys, and troops of Apache scouts, as well trained as he was, merciless, and ready to shoot on sight, scoured the countryside.

The trail of the escapees led east, and, although on foot, they moved fast. On the fifth of November, three days after their escape, Kid and Bach-e-on-al were seen on the San Carlos River, four miles from the agency, and about thirty-five miles from their escape on Kelvin Grade. There was an unsuccessful attempt to capture Kid and Bach-e-on-al, and it was learned that their wives were missing. The same day, the governor offered $500 for the capture and conviction of one or more of the escapees, and Sheriff Ryan offered $50 per man. A few days later, Sergeant of Scouts Rowdy and his men chased Kid and the others from a cave on the Salt River, but they found only Middleton's overcoat. Then the renegades disappeared for six months, most likely south into the Sierra Madre, some of the roughest country in the world but having small hidden villages of Apaches in deep vertical canyons.

In late April of 1890, a scout, Josh, claimed he heard a rumor on the reservation that the renegades might be hiding in the Ash Flat country of Graham County. He led troops there, who surprised and killed four, Hale, Bach-e-on-al, Has-ten-tu-du-jay, and Bi-the-ja-tish-to-ce-an, in a running gunfight.

In May of 1890, the infamous Mexican colonel Kosterlitsky with Mexican Rurales following bandits discovered that Apaches had killed the bandits. Trailing the Apaches, the Rurales killed three. Kosterlitsky discovered Sheriff Reynolds's revolver and watch on the body of one old man with long, gray hair. By now nearly every crime committed in southern Arizona was being attributed to Kid and the others.

The chase for the renegades grew hot, crowded, and determined. By late June, a lieutenant at Fort Bowie had sent out fifty-seven details that had covered a distance of about fifteen thousand miles for the month in southern Arizona looking for the renegades. For unknown reasons, Kid and the remaining three renegades decided to part company. Phyllis de la Garza believes it's likely Kid joined forces with Massai, who had escaped the train carrying Geronimo, and the Chiricahuas on the way to Florida.

In the summer of 1890, the renegades, without Kid, were hiding in the Mescal Creek area near the Gila River and about twenty miles from San Carlos. Hos-cal-te decided he had to see his family and had a happy reunion with them and friends until Say-es and El-cahn appeared, threatening them all and demanding food. When Hos-cal-te's father-in-law tried to send them away, Say-es killed him with Hunkydory Holmes's revolver. A remorseful Hos-cal-te, blaming himself for the death of his father-in-law, surrendered to the army and told where the others were hiding.

After a short fight, El-cahn, unarmed, was killed, and Say-es, out of ammunition and wounded in the arm, surrendered. On October 15, Say-es was sentenced to life imprisonment at Yuma for the murder of Reynolds and Holmes, and Hos-cal-te to his original sentence of twelve years. Say-es died of tuberculosis in the Yuma Territorial Prison on March 29, 1894, and Hos-cal-te the next day from the same disease.

By late October 1890, all the renegades escaping at Kelvin Grade, except Apache Kid, had been killed or caught and were awaiting trial.

By the end of November 1892, a combination of rewards from Gila County ($500), Graham County ($500), Arizona Territory ($5,000), Arizona Cattleman's Association ($2,000), New Mexico Territory ($2,000), and Porfirio Diaz, president of Mexico ($5,000), amounted to a total of $15,000 for proof-positive of the Apache Kid being killed or captured. None of these rewards were ever claimed or paid.

In the years that followed, there were many reports of the Kid stealing women and cattle and killing enemies, but the evidence was thin. There were also claims of him being killed, but these, too, were often disputed. There are reports by those who knew him that Kid lived in Mexico well into the 1930s. Truly, Kid lived up to his Apache name Has-kay-bay-nay-ntayl, "Brave and tall and will come to a mysterious end."

MASSAI—THE WARRIOR WHO ESCAPED

Massai is famous among the Apaches for escaping from the train carrying the reservation Chiricahuas to a prisoner of war camp in Florida. It is believed that after his escape he sometimes rode with Apache Kid. Burt Lancaster played Massai in the 1954 movie *Apache*. While the movie told a good story, much of the historical Massai story is different.[1]

Massai's Early Life

Massai was a Chiricahua Apache born on Mescal Mountain near Globe, Arizona. He was the son of White Cloud and Little Star. His training was typical of most Apache boys. White Cloud taught him from the time he could practically walk to use a bow and, later, the spear and to go for long periods of time without food or water. He trained to run holding water in his mouth to ensure he breathed through his nose, and, by the time he was nine years old, he could run to the top of Mescal Mountain and back. Then White Cloud made him run up the mountain carrying a pack of stones. White Cloud gradually increased the pack weight until Massai could run the distance carrying a very heavy load. After Massai's fitness development, he was trained in horsemanship in which his daughter says he excelled. White Cloud trained Massai in rifle marksmanship by making him shoot through an iron ring hung from a tree limb. When he missed, he was sent to his mother in disgrace. As he became a proficient marksman, shooting through the iron ring from a given distance, the distance was increased again until he could consistently shoot through the iron ring at one hundred yards.

In those days, Gray Lizard, a Tonkawa boy, was Massai's closest friend. Gray Lizard and his parents had come from the plains to the east and had joined the band White Cloud helped support. Gray Lizard and Massai trained and hunted together and caught and broke wild horses. In their mid-teen years, they began their novitiate to become warriors.

Before their novitiate was completed, Geronimo visited the ranchería of their band to speak with the warriors in council. He asked the warriors to join him in fighting the White Eyes. Geronimo believed the Apaches had to drive the White Eyes away before their numbers became so large they would overwhelm any resistance. He claimed that Mangas Coloradas was killed when he asked for peace, that Cochise had died of a broken heart because he foresaw his people being wiped out, and that the sons of Mangas Coloradas and Cochise did nothing because they saw what happened to their fathers. In Apache societies, the warriors didn't have to follow a chief. Individuals were free to decide to follow Geronimo, and a number did.

C. S. Fly photograph of Massai, a scout on the San Carlos Reservation, ca. 1880
PHOTO COURTESY OF NATIONAL ARCHIVES

Although not yet finished with their novitiate to become warriors, Massai and Gray Lizard wanted to follow Geronimo. They asked permission from their fathers and were told they were almost men and it was their decision to make, so they chose to follow Geronimo. Geronimo told them the time for wiping out the White Eyes wasn't ripe and that it might take more than two harvests (two years) before he and his followers were ready to fight. He told them to prepare by making caches of supplies—food, clothes, moccasins, cooking pots, and ammunition—and that they would strike when they had enough supplies to last many months. Although many didn't plan to join Geronimo in making war on the White Eyes, his idea of preparing for times of war was a good one, and many began the work. With so much taking and storing of food, game, and other food, sources grew scarce. Massai and Gray Lizard asked permission from their fathers to go far in search of meat and hides. Their fathers let them go. Each leading a packhorse, they went far enough west that they could see the big water. They took so much venison that, after loading their packhorses, they had to cache the remainder in the cave where they had camped.

When Massai and Gray Lizard returned to Mescal Mountain, they learned that those who wanted to follow Geronimo had gone to Ojo Caliente, the reservation and home of Victorio and Loco's Warm Springs Apaches (Mimbreños). Continuing on to Ojo Caliente, they discovered that Geronimo had been arrested and taken to San Carlos along with the Mimbreños and their leaders. Chiricahua scouts working for the army caught Massai and Gray Lizard and carried them to San Carlos. Massai and Gray Lizard spoke with Geronimo, who told them to be patient and await his word to break out. All the while, Geronimo schemed and planned, recruited warriors, and took ammunition from soldiers.

Massai married a Chiricahua girl at San Carlos, and they had two children. In these years, he became a scout and was photographed around 1880 at least once with Apache Kid and Rowdy (who won a Medal of Honor in 1890 for heroism in a fight with Kid and others), who were scouts at that time. At the prodding of Geronimo and other Chiricahua leaders, the White Eyes moved the Chiricahuas and Mimbreños from their desolate San Carlos camps to Turkey Creek near Fort Apache, and times were peaceful. Turkey Creek was in mountainous country with good water, grass, and plenty of game. When belief in rumors that he was about to be hanged drove Geronimo and his followers to break out in 1885, Massai, like many Chiricahuas, stayed with his family on the reservation.

Massai and Gray Lizard Escape from the Florida Train for Prisoners of War

GERONIMO AND OTHERS LEFT THE RESERVATION IN 1885 AND BEGAN RAIDING OUT OF the Sierra Madre from camps in Sonora and Chihuahua. Massai, who like 70 percent of the Chiricahuas, stayed on the reservation and refused to participate in Geronimo's war.

After failing to capture Geronimo, Gen. Nelson A. Miles, who replaced Gen. George Crook, recommended to the Departments of the Army and Interior that all Chiricahuas, including those who had not left the reservation, be rounded up and kept wherever the government decided to keep Geronimo and his people. Surprisingly, the two bureaucracies, competing for oversight of the reservations, agreed. Then, within a day after Geronimo surrendered, Miles ordered all of the reservation Chiricahuas scooped up and sent to Florida.

The normal procedure for supplying rations to Apache families on the reservation was for a member of the family to pick up supplies at the agency once a week. Within days after Geronimo surrendered to General Miles, the Chiricahuas remaining at San Carlos were all asked to come to the agency for rations. Although suspicious something wasn't right, they went and were abruptly surrounded by soldiers and disarmed. The men were herded into a building, and the women and children sent to pack their belongings. Massai tried to stir up the men to revolt, but none would because they had no arms, were surrounded by soldiers, and their families were in army hands.

The next day, all the men and their families were loaded on wagons and driven ninety miles in five days north to Holbrook. There they, along with the scouts who were still in the employment of the army, were put on a train on September 13, 1886. Ten cars were loaded with the Apaches. At the front and rear of the ten Apache cars was a car for the military escort of eight officers and eighty-four enlisted men. On the platforms between each two cars of prisoners four soldiers (two on each car platform) were on guard around the clock. All the doors and windows of the cars were fastened shut. The only toilet facilities were buckets at each end of each car. It's not hard to imagine what the heat and stench

Katherine Taylor Dodge photograph of Issue Day at the San Carlos Reservation, ca. 1899
PHOTO COURTESY OF LIBRARY OF CONGRESS

inside those sealed cars must have been like traveling across the Southwest in late summer. Angie Debo in her biography of Geronimo suggests that this may have been where the Apaches, normally very clean people, might have picked up the tubercular infection that wiped out nearly 25 percent of them during their first three and a half years in captivity. The Apaches expected to be killed at any time, and the soldiers, knowing this, had their fun by doing hand slashes in front of their necks indicating throats to be cut whenever they had the opportunity.

Massai decided to escape. His wife, knowing she could not leave their children and that she would probably never see Massai again if he got away, urged Massai and Gray Lizard to go. They spent three days loosening a fastened window when guards were not watching. They knew they would have to go through the window when the train was going slow up a long grade, otherwise they would never survive landing at train speeds on the flats or going downhill. (Mangas, on the way to Florida in late October, tried jumping out a window when the train was moving through Colorado. He was stunned but unhurt and easily recaptured.)

As the train approached Missouri, Massai and Gray Lizard saw mountains low on the horizon to the east and knew that soon they would probably be headed up a grade where they could jump. When food was brought for the noon meal, Massai and Gray Lizard pretended to eat and saved their portions, and Massai's wife gladly gave her share to Massai, knowing she would get more that night.

The train began laboring up a slope, going ever slower. Massai looked for a place grown thick with brush and trees, and as the train crawled almost to a stop nearing the top of a hill, Massai and Gray Lizard were through the window and rolling down the grade slope into the thick brush, where they stayed unmoving as the train slowly disappeared over the top of the hill. They wiggled through the brush and found a place to hide until dark. When they thought it safe to move, they headed for low mountains to the southwest, hoping to find Indians who would help them. They reached the low mountains and rested, but they found only White Eye farms and settlements. The next evening they found a miners' camp, and the next day, when the miners all went off to work, Massai and Gray Lizard crept into the camp, took repeating rifles, knives, and all the ammunition they could find and cut some meat from a dressed sheep carcass hanging from a tree.

Traveling mostly at night, they headed west. They killed a deer, carried all the meat they could, and used the deer's stomach, which they had cleaned, for a water bag. Unfortunately, Gray Lizard, who was carrying the water, fell against a prickly pear and tore a hole in the bag. They hoped to make another from an antelope but didn't see any. Massai and Gray Lizard both made medicine by praying to *Ussen* as they walked and ran west, thirsty and hungry. *Ussen* heard their prayers and sent a strong rain. Massai and Gray Lizard dug a hole in the ground to catch the water, and after drinking as much as they could, they continued west, following the stars. After a long, hard trek, they came to a river flowing with sour, alkaline water and knew they had reached the Río Pecos in eastern New Mexico. The next morning they could see what appeared to be a dark cloud on the western horizon and realized they were seeing the tops of the Capitan Mountains. Thanking *Ussen*, they made their way to forests on the mountain slopes.

Massai and Gray Lizard made a camp in the Capitans and rested for a day after taking a deer and feasting. Moving on, they crossed Capitan Gap and went around the great White Mountain, Sierra Blanca, in the land of the Mescaleros. Gray Lizard wanted to continue on to their home at Mescal Mountain, but Massai knew it was the first place army scouts would come looking and refused to go. They talked over whether to go or stay and decided to part ways. Gray Lizard went to Mescal Mountain, and Massai stayed around Sierra Blanca. The last Massai ever saw of his friend Gray Lizard was his descent from the ridge above Three Rivers into the Tularosa Basin heading west toward the White Sands and San Andres Mountains. Massai went down the other side of the mountain and made a camp in a Rinconada valley cave high on Sierra Blanca.

As Massai had suspected when he parted ways with Gray Lizard, the army and tribal police came looking for him at Mescal Mountain. However, his first wife, a prisoner with the Chiricahua families in Florida, and others had given a false description of Massai to the army, describing him as a big man about the size of Chief Naiche. When the tribal police went looking for Massai at Mescal Mountain, they found no one the size of Naiche and went away without his capture.

The distance Massai and Gray Lizard covered on foot using only their woodcraft skills and navigating by the stars is believed to have been at least six hundred miles, but it was probably more like nine hundred miles and over country they had never seen before.

Massai Takes a New Wife

MASSAI LIVED FREE, AND GAME WAS PLENTIFUL IN THE RINCONADA. HE USED A BOW TO hunt rather than his rifle to avoid alerting potential army hunters from nearby Fort Stanton. Although Massai had plenty to eat and hides to keep warm, he was very lonely. One morning he saw two Mescalero women and their children make a camp not far from his cave while they gathered piñon nuts. He watched them for three days and when no men appeared, he hid in the brush next to their camp and in the evening asked permission to enter their camp. Startled at first, they realized he was Apache and would respect them. They invited him to come and eat. He had already eaten but said he had not tasted coffee for a long time. They gave him some in a gourd, and he drank it slowly, savoring it. They visited with him, and he learned they were sisters. One was married to Scout Bigmouth. When Massai left, they gave him all the coffee they had. He didn't return to their camp or visit any of the others who came to harvest the piñons.

Massai waited until he believed all the piñon nut gatherers had left the Rinconada and then went hunting. He hid near a game trail that went to a large pool in a stream where he knew deer came to drink. He heard a splash in the pool. Looking to see what made the noise, Massai saw three young women bathing. He didn't move. It was ancient tribal law that spying on women was punishable by death. He watched fascinated as the girls bathed, left the pool, dressed, and began braiding their hair. It came to him that since under tribal law his life was forfeit anyway, he might as well take one of the girls. Suddenly appearing from his hiding place, he startled them, and they froze in place.

"Come!" he said to the first girl, but she begged him not to take her. She said, "My baby will die." He turned to the next, who stared wide-eyed, her wet braids so long they reached the ground. He picked up a braid and motioned for her to walk in front of him. The other two followed, begging him not to take her. When he turned and growled, "Shall I take you instead?" they ran away.

Massai took the captive to his cave, took her knife, cut pieces of rawhide, and tied her there. He left blankets, food, and water within easy reach for her, while he slept at the mouth of the cave. The next morning, wanting to get beyond tribal police pursuit he

1873 Timothy O'Sullivan photograph of an Apache warrior and his wife
PHOTO COURTESY OF LIBRARY OF CONGRESS

knew must come, he packed his supplies on a horse he had caught and tamed, freed the girl, and motioned her to make ready to travel. They walked beside the packhorse over the ridge between the Rinconada and Three Rivers down to the trail across the Tularosa Basin that ran between the ancient black lava flow called the Malpais (also known as the Valley of Fires) and White Sands to the San Andres Mountains. They camped and rested near a spring Massai knew in the foothills of the San Andres. He tied the girl to a tree while he hunted and told her that if she tried to escape, he would follow and kill her.

As they traveled, the girl gave him only yes or no answers to questions and never spoke otherwise. After a week Massai said, "Have I mistreated you?" She shook her head.

"Why, then, will you not talk to me?" She looked him in the eye and said, "You brought me by force. An Apache does not do that." He stared back at her. "Would you have come otherwise?" She tilted her chin up in defiance. "No!" He nodded. "Listen to me, then! It's true that I took you, but I have respected you. Now, unless you continue the journey to my people willingly, I will give you the horse and food. You will be free to return to your home. If you go to my people, my mother will make the wedding feast for us. It is for you to decide." She looked at the ground. "Which is it to be?" She looked in his eyes, saw he had a good heart, and said in a soft voice, "I will go with you."

The Mescalero girl's name was Zan-a-go-li-che, and for the rest of the way back to Mescal Mountain she rode the horse happy in the knowledge that Massai was a good man. Massai's mother made the promised wedding feast so that all the people of Mescal Mountain knew the couple was married.

Massai Goes to the Happy Place

THE YEARS PASSED. MASSAI AND ZAN-A-GO-LI-CHE HAD SIX CHILDREN. MASSAI HUNTED and raided, sometimes with Apache Kid, to feed his family and was probably blamed for many more raids than he actually carried out. He stayed near Mescal Mountain until a Mexican friend of the family, old Santos, passed away, this after *Ussen*, the great Creator God of the Apaches, had warned Massai to leave earlier. With the passing of Santos, Massai took his family to hide in the backcountry. Game was scarce, and Massai had little luck hunting to feed his family. He decided to return to Zan-a-go-li-che's family in Mescalero. One morning as Massai went to his hidden place for their horses, a White Eye tried to ambush him. Massai killed the White Eye, but the White Eye's horse got away. Massai knew it would be only a matter of time before soldiers and cowboys followed the horse's trail back to him.

Massai told his family that *Ussen* had told him clearly he would not return to Mescalero. He told Zan-a-go-li-che and his oldest son, later to be called Albert, that they were a day's travel from the Mexican village named San Marcial on the Río Grande, and that if he, Massai, did not return with the horses the next morning, then they were to leave the horses and go at once to the village. They could walk during the day because the underbrush was thick, and they would not be seen. They were to hide in the brush outside San Marcial until dark and then go to a house with no man or big boy, tap on the door, and ask for help in the language of Santos. Massai gave his son directions on how to reach the Rinconada from San Marcial. From the Rinconada, Zan-a-go-li-che would know how to reach her family. Massai ordered his family to stay on the Mescalero Reservation.

The next dawn, Zan-a-go-li-che and her daughters heard gunshots. With the coming of daylight, Albert returned after following Massai to the horses. He told his mother that White Eyes had shot Massai as he was reaching for his horse. Albert said Massai told him to run and that they must leave immediately as Massai had directed. Zan-a-go-li-che refused to go until she knew Massai was dead. She believed death was better than being a captive of the White Eyes. All day from the edge of a mesa, Zan-a-go-li-che and her children watched a large camp of White Eyes.

Apache mother and child, Edward Curtis photograph, ca. 1904
PHOTO COURTESY OF LIBRARY OF CONGRESS

Scouts from the camp fanned out in all directions and came straggling back at the end of the day. The White Eyes made a great fire that they kept burning all night. The next morning there was a thick fog. When the fog lifted, there were no White Eyes, no horses, and a little smoke.

Zan-a-go-li-che was determined to go to the camp and bury Massai, but she and the family waited and watched all day to be sure the White Eyes weren't waiting in ambush. Early the next morning Zan-a-go-li-che left the children and baby still on a cradleboard with the oldest girl, who was about twelve, while she and Albert crept down to the abandoned camp and its still smoldering fire. Zan-a-go-li-che stirred the fire's ashes and found charred bones and laid them to one side in a little heap. She tried to get every fragment but found no remnant of a skull. She did find an ammunition belt buckle and recognized it as Massai's by a dent made by a deflected bullet. She fastened the buckle to her belt and carefully wrapped the bones in her shawl.

Zan-a-go-li-che and Albert scraped out a hole with their hands and a sharp stone and buried Massai's remains. They heaped stones on the grave and left Massai to make the journey to the Happy Place. He went with no weapons, no horse, and no body, but Zan-a-go-li-che knew *Ussen* would understand that an Apache and a brave warrior came to him.

The family made it to San Marcial. There were men at every house except one, that of an old woman at the edge of town. She welcomed them in. She had little food, but she helped Zan-a-go-li-che find temporary homes with Mexican families for three of the girls. Massai's daughter, Alberta, who was about four years old at the time, was placed with the family of the Anglo railroad station agent.

Zan-a-go-li-che with the baby on the cradleboard and Albert made their way back to Mescalero and the home of her brother, Marion Simms. At first he didn't recognize her, but after she shared childhood stories only she could have known, Marion took her and the two children to the Mescalero agent, James A. Carroll. When Zan-a-go-li-che told Mr. Carroll the whereabouts of her other children, he took Marion, who spoke excellent English, to the Tularosa train station, bought him a round-trip ticket to San Marcial via El Paso, and gave him $10.00 to buy food.

At San Marcial, the three Mexican families were happy to return the children to their mother. The station agent, the only Anglo in town, wanted to keep Alberta because his family had grown attached to her and he had spent considerable money on her in the way of food and clothes. But the child begged and pleaded to return. The agent finally agreed to let her go if he could get back the money he had spent on her. Marion had less than ten dollars in his pocket, all that was left of the money Mr. Carroll had given him for food. He gave every penny to the agent and boarded the train to Tularosa with Alberta and the other children.

When the children returned, Zan-a-go-li-che took them to the agency to be enrolled. They all sat on the floor in a circle while, with Marion translating, information was gathered as to names and approximate ages. The wife of the clerk, Ms. Jefferis, noticed that one by one the children were stealthily taking and eating bits of food from their mother's buckskin emergency bag. As Ms. Jefferis walked around the circle, she found that the starved children were eating dried grasshoppers. Ms. Jefferis soon made sure the children and Zan-a-go-li-che had all the food they could eat.

Apache Prisoners of War

The Chiricahua and Mimbreño Apaches had broken out of the hellhole called San Carlos Reservation several times, following such leaders as Victorio, Nana, Naiche, and Geronimo. Each time they had come back willingly or had been forced back after surrender to General Crook, who made efficient and effective use of Apache scouts to track the escapees and talk them into returning. When Geronimo left San Carlos the third time in 1885, only about 30 percent of the Chiricahua and Mimbreño Apaches went out with him and leaders such as Naiche, Chihuahua, Mangas, and Nana. Nevertheless, when Gen. George Crook was forced to resign after Geronimo failed to come in as he promised, Gen. Nelson A. Miles, appointed as Crook's replacement, sent all the Chiricahuas and Mimbreños, including scouts and others who had peaceably stayed on the reservation, into exile in prisoner of war camps in Florida.

In the years that followed, Geronimo, Naiche, Mangas, and their followers first lived at Fort Pickens near Pensacola, Florida. The rest of the prisoners lived at Fort Marion at Saint Augustine, Florida. The families of Geronimo, Naiche, and Mangas were kept at Saint Augustine for about six months before they were reunited with their men at Fort Pickens while the rest of the prisoners were sent on to the Mount Vernon Barracks north of Mobile, Alabama. The most educationally promising Apache children were separated from their parents and sent to Carlisle School in Pennsylvania.

Bureaucratic bungling initially left the Apaches in Florida with inadequate rations and close to starvation for several months, and many died from malaria and tuberculosis. In 1887 and 1888, they were transferred to Mount Vernon Barracks, but the death rate from disease continued to be about three times the national average. In the fall of 1894, they were all transferred to Fort Sill, Oklahoma, where they built villages, farmed, raised cattle, and lived peaceably. Most of the famous warriors and chiefs, Nana, Chihuahua, Loco, and Mangas, died and were buried there. In 1909 Geronimo, who had become a national celebrity, caught pneumonia and died, prompting Washington bureaucrats to decide they could let the surviving prisoners go. In April 1913, most of the Chiricahuas and a few Mimbreños (some chose to remain at Fort Sill) were welcomed to the Mescalero Reservation to start their lives as free people, their long prisoner of war agony ended.

The stories in this section provide snapshots of the history and life and times endured by the Chiricahuas and Mimbreño Apaches during their years in captivity.

Apache Prisoners of War for Twenty-Seven Years

WHEN GERONIMO SURRENDERED AFTER HIS LAST SAN CARLOS BREAKOUT, HE HAD about thirty-five men, women, and children with him, and of these, about sixteen were warriors. These people were the small contingent that broke away from the main body of Chiricahua and Mimbreño Apaches surrendering in March of 1886 after Geronimo first accepted General Crook's terms for surrender, and then failed to come in as he promised. Geronimo finally surrendered on September 4, 1886. At that time there were a large number of Chiricahuas and others (several hundred) on the San Carlos Reservation who had peaceably stayed and had never left the reservation. These included Chiricahua army scouts who had helped General Crook find and persuade Geronimo to surrender in 1883 and 1885/1886.

President Grover Cleveland determined that all the Chiricahua and Mimbreño Apaches and others who had fought with Geronimo had to be brought east as prisoners of war to prevent any chance of further Apache uprisings. He wouldn't listen to the pleas of many military leaders (including General Crook) to let the scouts and peaceful Chiricahuas and Mimbreños stay where they were.

When Geronimo surrendered, there was a scramble to determine where to send the Chiricahuas. General Nelson Miles, who had replaced Crook after Geronimo failed to come in and had pushed the idea of sending all the Chiricahuas and Mimbreños east, suggested sending them to Kansas or the Comanche/Kiowa reservation in southern Oklahoma (now Fort Sill) where Quanah Parker lived, but a law (the Dawes Act) made that impossible, and in fact, the Comanche and Kiowa were avowed enemies of the Apaches.

The army had already sent the Chiricahuas who surrendered in March 1886 and some family members of Geronimo's breakaway group to Fort Marion in St. Augustine, Florida. The decision was made to send the breakaway warriors of Geronimo's group to Fort Pickens on Santa Rosa Island in the Florida panhandle near Pensacola, which separated them from their families.

About one-third of the Apaches died while in the south (their average death rate was three times the national average). The brightest children (twenty-four boys and fifteen

September 10, 1886, Apache prisoners of war at a rest stop beside Southern Pacific Railway, near the Nueces River, Texas, en route to Fort Pickens prisoner of war camp. Chief Naiche sits in the center of the first row with Geronimo at the place of honor to his left.
PHOTO COURTESY OF NATIONAL ARCHIVES

girls) were taken from their parents and sent to the Indian School at Carlisle, Pennsylvania, for training. Within two years, twelve children, dying from tuberculosis, were returned to their parents. In April 1887, living conditions were so bad in Florida that public pressure forced the government to send most of the families to Mount Vernon Barracks, a deserted army arsenal about twenty-eight miles north of Mobile. By January 1888, it was already clear and all agreed that Mount Vernon Barracks was an unsuitable place to keep the prisoners—the environment was unhealthy, land was too poor to farm, and there was nothing for them to do—and a search had begun for a new place. In May 1888, the Apaches at Fort Pickens, who had lost no one to disease, were also sent to Mount Vernon Barracks. The Cherokees in western North Carolina agreed to sell 12,000 acres of their reservation to the Chiricahuas, but there were loud local objections to that, and the area was too small for the Apaches to support themselves living there. The army even investigated two sites for starting a reservation in the Tidewater area of Virginia, but these, too, were rejected for being too small.

General Crook met with the Apaches in January 1890. He then held press conferences in Washington where, as one reporter claimed, Crook aroused sympathy for a suffering people and indignation against the authors of "a perfidious and heartless wrong." Years of political maneuvering followed until August 1894 when the Apaches were loaded on a train and sent to Fort Sill, Oklahoma—the place for them that General Crook had been fighting for all along.

Objections were raised to sending them to Fort Sill, and it was claimed the Apaches had misled Crook at the Mount Vernon meeting when they said all they wanted was a place of their own to leave peaceably and support themselves. Crook replied that there was no probability that the Apaches would turn "like snakes upon the government. The Apaches are broken in spirit and humbled to the dust."

In 1911, six Apaches and two army officers went to New Mexico to look for sites where the Fort Sill Apaches could resettle after being released as prisoners of war. The Mescaleros offered to share their reservation with them and the offer was accepted. In the spring of 1913, the Apache prisoners of war were released. Of these, 127 moved to New Mexico, but 87 stayed behind on farms they had built up over the years.

The United States, its politicians and bureaucrats, frightened that the Apaches might reappear as the warriors they once were, had held them as prisoners of war for twenty-seven years until all their finest war leaders had passed away.

Apache Prisoners of War at Mount Vernon Barracks

MOUNT VERNON BARRACKS, ABOUT TWENTY-EIGHT MILES NORTH OF MOBILE, ALA-
bama, which held the Apache prisoners of war for over seven years, was the location of
their second quarters. Fort Pickens on Santa Rosa Island in Pensacola Bay and Fort Marion at St. Augustine, Florida, held them for over a year and were the first sites to which
they were sent.[1]

Over 70 percent of the Chiricahuas and Mimbreños stayed on their reservation when
Geronimo broke out in 1885 with 35 men, 8 boys old enough to bear arms, and 101
women and children, 144 all told. After General Miles recommended all the Chiricahuas
and some Mimbreños (Warm Springs) be grouped in one place, the government shipped
394 (including scouts still on the army payroll) to already crowded Fort Marion, which
held 70 from the group that initially surrendered to General Crook in March 1886. When
Geronimo and about sixteen warriors, wives, and their children, about thirty all told,
finally surrendered in September 1886, the warriors were shipped to Fort Pickens, and
their families, to Fort Marion.

In Florida, Apache children selected for education at the Carlisle Industrial School
run by General Pratt were taken from their parents and shipped north to Carlisle, Pennsylvania. However, it wasn't long before several of the children were returned to Fort
Marion or Mount Vernon Barracks with tuberculosis.

Fort Marion Apaches soon began dying from starvation, resulting from bureaucratic
mismanagement of ration allotments at the War Department, and malaria and yellow
fever from mosquitoes, and tuberculosis. The death rate was so high and General Crook
made such a point of it in national newspapers, that public outrage forced the War
Department to look for a healthier place to keep the prisoners. After a number of false
starts, Mount Vernon Barracks was selected, and the Fort Marion Apaches were shipped
there. On the way the train stopped on April 27, 1887, and let the families of the warriors
held at Fort Pickens join them. The reunited Fort Pickens families were later shipped to
Mount Vernon a year later on May 13, 1888. During the year they were at Fort Pickens,
only one died, Geronimo's wife She-ga, who was ill before she arrived in Florida.

Apache leaders at Mount Vernon Barracks, ca. 1890. Left to right are Chihuahua, Naiche, Loco, Nana, and Geronimo.
PHOTO COURTESY OF NATIONAL ARCHIVES

Mount Vernon Barracks, with 2,160 acres of land surrounded by pine forest and swamps, was much larger than Fort Marion. Eugene Chihuahua reported that when they arrived from Fort Marion, the married couples were placed in tumbledown houses with dirt floors and the unmarried men were housed together. It rained all the time, and the roofs leaked. Fort Marion had been bad, but Mount Vernon, hot and steamy, with its rain and mosquitoes, was worse. Literally everything molded—food, clothes, even moccasins. The clouds of mosquitoes soon led to the shaking sickness (malaria) for many. Dr. Walter Reed, who was researching how malaria and yellow fever were transmitted, visited Mount Vernon Barracks while the Apaches were there.

The Apache men were set to cutting down trees and building houses with roofs that were sufficient for keeping them dry and more comfortable. The log cabins were built with two rooms, each about ten feet square, with an open "dogtrot" porch under a roof in between to help cool them. These new cabins also had dirt floors, and the Apaches slept on the dirt or boards, cooked over open fires, and sat on the ground. Sibley stoves provided some heat, but they had no chimneys. When Geronimo and his band arrived from Fort Pickens, more cabins had to be built. The cabin layout was ideal for Geronimo, who kept his wife Zi-yeh and her son Fenton in one room and his wife Ih-tedda and her daughter Lenna in the other.

Nana, based on what General Crook had originally offered in March 1886 (two years in exile in Florida before returning to their homeland), continued to advise the people to not antagonize their captors. He said they could make it through two years of captivity. When the years passed and it became obvious they weren't going to be freed, he still encouraged them to stay calm and survive.

The commander at Fort Marion was so impressed with Chihuahua (the soldiers, impressed with his manners and dignity, nicknamed him "Chesterfield") that he told him he would not have to work if he agreed to wear a full captain's uniform as a leader of his people. Chihuahua thought wearing pants was degrading but agreed to wear the uniform after cutting the seat out of the trousers so he could still wear his breechcloth.

The Massachusetts Indian Association, a philanthropic friend of the Indians association, raised money and sent two teachers for the Apache children at Mount Vernon after convincing the Apaches they weren't going to steal the children and send them somewhere else. These women, beginning in the winter and early spring of 1889, taught eighty pupils the first year in a one-room building furnished by the post. Geronimo enthusiastically supported the school, recognizing the importance of the White Eye skills gained from what could be learned in the school. He apparently appointed himself as the school's disciplinarian, spending much time with the children and training them with the same strict discipline he used in preparing boys to become warriors in earlier years.

The death rate of the Apaches pushed the government to relocate them again. General Howard, who had negotiated the treaty with Cochise fifteen years earlier, ordered a detailed report on the status of the Apache prisoners of war at Mount Vernon Barracks. General Howard's aide de camp, his son, Lt. Guy Howard, signed the report. The report showed that of the 498 Apaches imprisoned between April 13, 1886, and November 7, 1886, 129 (26 percent) had died in the following three years: 49 at Fort Marion, 50 at Mount Vernon, and 30 at Carlisle. Eighty-one babies had been born during the same time, leaving a total number of 460 still alive. The report stated that the expected death rate for "civilized" people was 2 percent per annum but that of the Apaches, including those sent to Carlisle, was 6.8 percent.

Nearly all the Carlisle deaths were originally attributed to the high humidity causing tuberculosis (this is what Walter Reed believed). However, it was later determined that about ten years before the Apache children arrived at Carlisle, plains Indian children who were suffering from the disease (apparently infected by white traders) had been sent to Carlisle. Before these Indians died or were sent back home, they left enough traces of the disease to still infect many of the Apache children who had not been exposed to the deadly lung disease. Geronimo, believing that with the next change of command the Apaches would be executed, sent his married, twenty-two-year-old son, Chappo, who had ridden with him during the last breakout, to Carlisle, where he thought Chappo would be safe. Chappo returned to Mount Vernon after six years at Carlisle and soon died from tuberculosis. Lozen, legendary warrior woman, although never going to Carlisle, is believed to have died from the disease in June of 1890.

After General Crook had inspected more appropriate sites on which to locate the Apaches, it was decided that Fort Sill was the best place for them. In January of 1890, after reading the reports from Howard and Crook, President Harrison "earnestly" recommended to Congress "provision be made by law for locating them upon lands in the Indian Territory" (southern Oklahoma). Unfortunately, Harrison's request had bad political timing. The Apache prisoners had to wait another three years before Congress enacted legislation that allowed them to be moved to Fort Sill, which was a military reservation, thereby evading Dawes Act prohibitions against the settlement of southwest Indians in the Indian Territory.

Mescaleros Sent to Florida with the Chiricahuas Get an Early Release

THE MESCALERO RESERVATION BECAME THE HOME OF THE CHIRICAHUA PRISONERS OF war released from Fort Sill in April 1913. When the army swept up the Chiricahuas at Fort Apache in 1886 for shipment to Florida, several Mescaleros with Chiricahua connections were also taken, even though they were totally innocent of Geronimo's raids (in fact this was true of 75 percent of the Chiricahuas, not including the scouts who had helped the army track Geronimo) prior to his surrender in September 1886.

The Mescaleros on the reservation urged the government to release their people, and the War Department agreed they could return to Mescalero. Twelve were released in February 1889 (more than two years after Geronimo surrendered). Among them was Geronimo's Mescalero wife, Ih-tedda, and their little daughter, Lenna.

After Geronimo had broken out of San Carlos the third time in May of 1885, the army moved his family, who had not left with him, along with other Chiricahuas, and kept them under close guard for their own protection at Fort Apache, so they couldn't be forced to join Geronimo's band hiding in the Sierra Madre. Geronimo and four warriors, who had wives at Fort Apache, decided to take them back. They traveled on foot through the mountains and slipped past the watchful eyes of White Mountain Apache scouts patrolling the country. Geronimo and the warriors found the camp of Geronimo's family, took back his wife She-ga and their three-year-old daughter, and stole another woman, Bi-ya-neta. They also took some White Mountain ponies before they faded away into the eastern mountains. Perico, one of Geronimo's most able warriors, unable to take his wife back, took Bi-ya-neta. Perico and Bi-ya-neta were together the rest of their lives in the Sierra Madre, in prisoner of war captivity, and after their release. They had five children, three of whom are buried at Fort Sill.

On their way back from the raid on Fort Apache, Geronimo's warriors found a small group of Mescalero women who had been allowed to leave the reservation with a larger party to collect piñon nuts and hunt deer in the southwestern mountains of New Mexico. Among them was a woman, Cumpah, later known as Sara, her young son, later named

1892 photograph of Ih-tedda, Lenna, and Robert Geronimo. Ih-tedda by the time of this photograph was married to a retired scout, Old Boy, and had the name Katie Cross Eyes. Lenna was always understood to be Geronimo's daughter. For several years Robert was believed to be the son of Old Boy until Katie admitted his father was actually Geronimo.

PHOTO COURTESY OF THE LYNDA SÁNCHEZ/EVE BALL COLLECTION

Charlie Smith, a woman with a baby, and an unmarried girl later named Ih-tedda (Young Girl). The warriors scooped them up, placed each one on a horse behind a warrior, and carried them to Geronimo's camp. Geronimo took Ih-tedda for a wife. Other warriors took the other two women.

When Geronimo, a prisoner at the Mount Vernon Barracks living with She-ga, Ih-tedda, and their children, learned in early 1889 that Mescaleros were being released back to the Mescalero Reservation, he told Ih-tedda she had to leave him and go back to Mescalero. She said she loved him and didn't want to go. Geronimo told her he believed the Chiricahuas might be shot at any time and that to save her life and their daughter Lenna's, she must return to Mescalero. Ih-tedda reluctantly agreed. In Apache culture, when a married woman returned to the home of her mother, she was considered divorced and free to remarry. A few days after Ih-tedda and Lenna returned to Mescalero, her parents, against her wishes, married her to Old Cross Eyes, a retired scout living on a pension of eight dollars a month. From that time, her name was Katie Cross Eyes, and her husband was called Old Boy. In August of that year, seven months later, Katie gave birth to a son and listed his name at the agency as Robert Cross Eyes.

In 1904, fifteen years later, Lenna, representing Mescalero Apaches at the St. Louis Exposition, was delighted to meet her father, Geronimo, where he was among those representing the Chiricahua Apaches. Later that year Robert went to the Indian School at Chilocco, Oklahoma, about two hundred miles north of Fort Sill. He still had the name Robert Cross Eyes. Katie, however, later requested his name be changed on the reservation records to Robert Geronimo.

When Asa Daklugie, Geronimo's nephew and son of Juh, learned that a boy at Chilocco claimed to be the son of Geronimo, he checked the date of his birth with the agency and told Geronimo, who said, "Well, he could be my son." A year later Robert visited with Geronimo at Fort Sill, and the old man was convinced the boy was his son. Geronimo's judgment in sending Ih-tedda back to Mescalero was vindicated by the fact that Lenna and Robert were his only children who lived to carry on the family.

Also among those returning to Mescalero was the boy, Charlie Smith, taken in the same group as Ih-tedda, and his parents. His father, Askadodilges (Hides His Foot), also named Charlie Smith, was the leader of the returning party. Once on the Mescalero Reservation, Askadodilges, who became known as "Alabama Charlie," returned to their home at White Tail. Askadodilges passed away during Charlie Smith's teen years, and Charlie hunted to support the family. Ammunition was expensive and he couldn't afford to waste a single shot. When asked if he took only one bullet when he went hunting, he is said to have answered, "I need only one deer." He also hunted mountain lion and lobos with one bullet.

Charlie Smith went to the Indian school at Albuquerque and was considered a good student. He served as a scout in Mexico during General Pershing's chase after Pancho Villa in 1916, was captured by Mexican cavalry, and served more than a year as a prisoner of war until prisoners were exchanged. He continued his career as an army scout under Gen. Omar Bradley and was famous for his marksmanship. In his later years he served as the chief of the Mescalero police force and a judge on the tribal court. He was a contributor to Morris Opler's books, *An Apache Lifeway* and *An Apache Odyssey, A Journey Between Two Worlds*. Charlie Smith, being full of years, passed away at Mescalero in 1973.

Apache Prisoners of War Sent to Fort Sill

THE CHIRICAHUAS WERE DYING OFF AT AN ALARMING RATE IN FLORIDA. WITHIN TWO years of captivity there, they were moved by the Department of the Army to Mount Vernon Barracks in the hope they would do better, but in fact they probably did worse. General Otis Howard ordered a report to get the facts on their survival and was greatly disturbed to learn, for example, that the Apache death rate during their first three years of captivity was over three times that of the national population. At about the same time, General Crook and others had been directed to find and recommend a new place for the Chiricahuas to have their own reservation. The only place that was big enough to sustain them was on land the Comanche and Kiowa had as their reservation in and around Fort Sill, Oklahoma.[1]

In 1890, after reading the reports from Generals Howard and Crook, President Harrison recommended to Congress that the Apaches be relocated to lands in the Indian Territory, i.e., the Comanche-Kiowa reservation. Unfortunately, responding to settler and rancher fears that Apache raiding and warfare would be imported from Arizona and New Mexico into Oklahoma, Congress had passed a law (Dawes Act) in 1879 that forbade New Mexico and Arizona Indians from having a reservation in the Indian Nations territory. After much bureaucratic haggling, the War Department agreed to settle the Apaches within the lands of Fort Sill military reservation after the Comanche and Kiowa, who did not like the Apaches, agreed they could come. The agreement the Comanche and Kiowa had with the War Department ensured that when the army left Fort Sill, the land would revert back to the original Comanche-Kiowa reservation. The arrangement for moving the Apaches to Fort Sill so angered its commander that he planned to build a palisaded pen and keep them corralled under guard.

When Lt. Hugh Lenox Scott (one day to be Chief of Staff and later Secretary of the Army) learned of this plan, he realized it would lead to prisoners running away with much more bloodshed than the 1885 breakout and told the departmental commander, General Miles. Miles went over the head of the Fort Sill commander and placed Lieutenant Scott in charge of the prisoners and soon transferred the commander to another post in the East.

GERONIMO

Naiche and Geronimo, Fort Sill, Oklahoma. Photograph left by Gen. Hugh Scott after he passed away.
PHOTO COURTESY OF NATIONAL ARCHIVES

After Congress agreed to let the Apaches go to Fort Sill, it allocated $15,000 for buildings, draft animals, livestock, necessary farming tools, seeds, and other articles needed to support the Apaches. In early October 1894, the Apaches were placed on a train that carried them by way of New Orleans and Fort Worth to Rush Springs, Oklahoma, where wagons waited to carry them the remaining thirty miles to Fort Sill. In all, 296 arrived at Fort Sill on October 4. About forty-five of their children remained at the Carlisle, Pennsylvania, or Hampton, Virginia, Indian schools. The arriving Apaches had no livestock, not even a dog or cat, and most of their possessions had been destroyed in an accidental fire in a railroad shed in New Orleans. Forgetting their old animosity, hundreds of Comanche, Kiowa, and Kiowa-Apaches came to meet them and tried to talk in the universal sign language of the plains. But the Apaches, used to living in the mountains and deserts, didn't understand the sign language. Lieutenant Scott took some Kiowa-Apaches to see them, but the dialects were too dissimilar for mutual understanding. Both sides finally produced boys educated at Carlisle and they communicated for their respective groups through English.

The Comanches, Kiowa, and Kiowa-Apaches hauled the Apaches to Cache Creek on Fort Sill. It was too late in the season to build houses, so the Apaches put up wickiups using saplings growing along the creek, Lieutenant Scott providing them with canvas for wickiup covers, food rations, and blankets. The next year they built two-room, vertical plank houses with dogtrot centers wide enough to pull a wagon through. There were deer in the woods around Cache Creek, and Scott allowed them to hunt.

The Apaches soon learned that mesquite trees grew in a grove about forty-five miles away. Mesquite beans and bread from mesquite bean flour were among their favorite foods, and they hadn't eaten any since their exile had begun more than eight years earlier. They asked Scott for permission to gather the mesquite beans, and he said they could go on noon Saturday if they were back to work by 7:00 a.m. on the following Monday. They took along a few horses to carry tents, supplies, and beans. They gathered three hundred bushels of mesquite bean pods, trotted the ninety-mile round-trip when they traveled, and were ready to work the following Monday morning.

There were no fences around the Fort Sill military reservation. Lieutenant Scott (soon to be Captain Scott in January of 1895) showed them a map of where they were and the possible ways the Mescaleros said they might travel back to the Southwest if they tried to escape. He warned them that he had army troops and supplies waiting along all the trails that led back to Mescalero, New Mexico, and if they tried to leave the reservation, the army and his friends, the Comanche, wouldn't hesitate to come after them. None tried to leave.

When the homes were built, they were located in villages so that friendly people lived close together, and scouts they disliked were kept separated. Captain Scott understood Apache social structure and let each chief, famous scout, or headman have a village far enough from the others that he and his followers had some privacy. The villages were strung out along Cache and Medicine Bluff Creeks.

Schooling for the Chiricahua children who had lost their Mount Vernon teachers in the move was provided through arrangements made by the Indian Office to place them in the boarding school for plains tribes at Anadarko, thirty-three miles away. The Chiricahuas didn't want the children to go, but they told Scott they had been there long enough to know the officer's orders had to be carried out. During the school term, mothers bought candy or some other treat for their children and trotted the sixty-six-mile round-trip to present it.

The adult men learned the techniques for raising range cattle. The autographed picture shown with this story was probably given to Captain Scott during one of his later visits to Fort Sill. After eight years at the Carlisle School, Daklugie, Geronimo's nephew, returned to the Chiricahuas in 1895. He had studied cattle husbandry at Carlisle. Scott put Daklugie in charge of the Chiricahua herd, and he did a superb job managing and improving it.

Many of the men had served in the infantry at Mount Vernon Barracks (Company I, Twelfth Infantry). At Fort Sill, most of them enlisted in the Seventh Cavalry, Custer's old regiment. In fact, the Seventh was Eugene Chihuahua's assignment when his step-grandfather, Geronimo, died.

Apache Prisoner of War Years at Fort Sill

THE APACHE PRISONERS WERE HELD FOR MORE THAN EIGHTEEN YEARS AT FORT SILL, which was the third place they were kept.[1] They arrived at Fort Sill in early October 1894 and immediately set to work making canvas-covered wickiups to get them through the winter. Schoolchildren were sent to the boarding school for the plains tribes about thirty miles away at Anadarko. Army captain Hugh Lenox Scott was in charge of their welfare and helped with providing canvas covers for the wickiups, blankets, and other supplies.

In the spring of 1895, Captain Scott let them select village sites. The villages were scattered along Cache and Medicine Bluff Creeks far enough apart for privacy but still close enough to walk to for a visit. The men began building picket-style (vertical posts set

Photograph of a Chiricahua village at Fort Sill, ca. 1900
PHOTO COURTESY OF LIBRARY OF CONGRESS

in a frame) houses that consisted of a dogtrot breezeway and a bedroom on either side under a common roof. In addition to lumber, Captain Scott also provided wire and posts for fencing around the Fort Sill perimeter (about 50 miles long, covering an area of about 150 square miles) and pastures for their cattle. Their first cattle were bought with funds Congress had appropriated for the move from Mount Vernon Barracks. To work cattle, the Apaches, superb horsemen, had to learn horse moves every cowboy knew in order to manage and work the herd. It was the best life the Chiricahua and Mimbreño Apache prisoners of war had had since Geronimo had surrendered in 1886. Eugene Chihuahua said that at least they could see mountains, hear coyotes, and smell the sage.

How the Apaches spent their time at Fort Sill can be seen through what happened to a few of the better-known ones. Eugene Chihuahua, son of Chief Chihuahua and brother of Ramona, who married Daklugie, was the only child of Chief Chihuahua who escaped being sent to Carlisle Industrial School. At Chief Chihuahua's request, Eugene worked for George Wratten, the interpreter who was with the Apaches from San Carlos all the way through their internment. Wratten ran the trading post for the prisoners of war and taught Eugene to read using labels on canned goods and to do arithmetic in order to fill store orders. Eugene was nearly grown when they moved to Fort Sill. He was big, strong, and quick and loved to play baseball. The soldiers soon had him on the Fort Sill baseball team, where he was a star. He became a scout in the Seventh Cavalry (Custer's old regiment) and met two Indian girls he had wanted to marry, but his father said no each time because it meant he would leave to become part of his wife's family, and Chihuahua had picked Eugene to follow him as chief. Chihuahua chose Viola Massai for Eugene's wife. Viola was the daughter of the warrior Massai, who had escaped from the train carrying the prisoners to Florida and is the subject of part 5, "Massai–The Warrior Who Escaped."

Viola, her sister, and her mother were the family Massai left behind when he escaped the train. Viola went to the Carlisle school with the other Apache children and knew Eugene's sister, Ramona, well. As Eugene told Eve Ball, he and Viola loved each other, but were never in love with each other as *Ussen* intended. They had six children, all of whom died young. Viola went back to Mescalero with Eugene in 1913, found relatives there, and died there.

Asa Daklugie, son of Juh, nephew of Geronimo, went back to his people at Fort Sill in 1895 after spending eight years at the Carlisle school. Juh and Chihuahua had promised Daklugie and Ramona Chihuahua to each other when they were very young. Ramona had returned from Carlisle earlier and was ready to marry as soon as Daklugie returned to their people.

Daklugie decided to wait until he could make a sufficient income to support a family. He went to George Wratten and told him of his years of study of cattle at Carlisle and said the herd he had seen at Fort Sill should be improved. He also told Wratten he was angry at the way he saw the Apache women were treated by soldiers who had them doing chores like washing laundry (Angie Debo suspects he learned respect for women at the Carlisle school, even though he disliked the White Eyes).

Wratten sent him to see Captain Scott, who was in charge of the Apaches at Fort Sill. Daklugie made no effort to conceal his dissatisfaction with conditions on the reservation and a scuffle followed. Captain Scott was a small man, Daklugie big and strong. Scott ran from his office, mounted his horse, and rode away. Daklugie waited at Scott's office more than an hour for the military police to come and take him away. When none came, he mounted his horse and rode to the trading post. Wratten told him Scott had stopped and wanted to know about this fellow who wanted to run the reservation. Wratten told him Daklugie was Geronimo's nephew just back from Carlisle and that he was deeply interested in the welfare of his people, didn't want to run the reservation, and knew more about raising cattle than anyone else on the reservation. He also explained that all the older chiefs had great respect for Daklugie, and he just wanted a job. After Wratten's explanation, Scott put Daklugie in charge of the cattle, and the herd grew in numbers and quality. When the Apaches left Fort Sill for Mescalero and had to sell the herd, it was considered one of the best in Oklahoma.

About a year after he arrived from Carlisle, Daklugie and Ramona were married in two ceremonies. The first ceremony with Ramona wearing a beautiful, beaded buckskin dress for the wedding feast was the Apache way. The second ceremony followed that of the White Eyes with a minister and signed paper and Ramona wearing a beautiful silk dress, which she had made.

When it became known that the Apaches might be released and allowed to return to New Mexico to stay at Mescalero, Daklugie got a pass, spent his own money for travel expenses, went to Washington to argue the Apache case for their freedom, and then went to Mescalero to determine its desirability for a move and concluded it would be a great place for a permanent home and to raise cattle.

After building his house, Geronimo, along with a number of the Apaches, began cultivating gardens, melon patches, and kafir corn and sorghum crops. Geronimo was reported to have been one of Captain Scott's best farmers, although Scott did not like the old man. In the first summer after their arrival at Fort Sill, the Apaches raised more than 250,000 melons and cantaloupes in their individual gardens and fields. During an August of 1895 or 1896, it was reported that the Apaches cut and bailed more than 350 tons of hay. The hay they didn't use for their cattle, they sold to the army and other ranchers.

Geronimo was a money-making machine. He was shown off at numerous expositions around the country and given a travel allowance that he usually saved. At the expositions, he made and sold bows and arrows, signed autographs or had his picture taken for a fee, and sold hats he wore and cut buttons off his clothes to sell. It is said that when he passed away in 1909, after twenty-three years of captivity, he had about $10,000 (about $117,000 in today's dollars) in the bank.

S. M. Barrett, superintendent of schools at Lawton, Oklahoma, near Fort Sill, wanted to do a book about Geronimo. To Daklugie's surprise, the old man agreed to tell his life story and asked Daklugie to be his interpreter. Daklugie and Geronimo had to consider many things. Daklugie believed that, as prisoners of war, any time there was a change in army command, the Apaches might all be massacred. There was a chance Barrett was a spy and was trying to get information not obtainable by any other means. In fact, the military tried to stop the project, and Barrett had to appeal to Roosevelt for approval. When they met, Geronimo dictating and Daklugie translating, Barrett took notes. Barrett couldn't write as fast as Daklugie spoke and had to depend on his memory for part of what Daklugie told him. As a result of Daklugie and Geronimo being very careful to avoid giving Barrett incriminating evidence on any of Geronimo's warriors and Barrett's memory and attempt to make what Geronimo told him consistent with existing accounts, Barrett's *Geronimo, His Own Story, The Autobiography of a Great Patriot Warrior*, has a number of errors and large places where the information is limited or practically nonexistent.

In the eighteen-plus years the Apaches were prisoners of war at Fort Sill, they continued their tribal dances and ceremonials; they grew one of the best, if not the best, cattle herd in Oklahoma; their young men became superb baseball players and athletes in other sports; and they grew gardens and large crops of kafir corn and sorghum. They annually cut hundreds of tons of thin prairie grass to sell and use as they needed, built the villages and houses in which they lived, married and had children, and served as soldiers in the U.S. Army. In 1913, four years after their old great chiefs and the great warrior Geronimo had all passed away, they were allowed to return to live with the Mescaleros in New Mexico, and there they prosper today.

Geronimo Asks President Theodore Roosevelt to Let His People Go

AT THE TURN OF THE LAST CENTURY, GERONIMO WAS THE MOST FAMOUS INDIAN IN THE United States. People flocked to the reservation, fairs, parades, and national expositions to see him and to buy his souvenirs. In 1905, Geronimo, his nephew Daklugie, who served as his interpreter, and other Apaches were invited to Theodore Roosevelt's inauguration on March 4, where Geronimo and other well-known First Nations chiefs rode in the inaugural parade. The government paid all travel expenses, including shipping their best horses, which would have been considered their best warhorses in the old days. Before he left for the inauguration, the government gave Geronimo $171 for travel expenses. He put $170 in the bank and left with $1.00 in his pocket. When he returned, he had a trunk full of new clothes, and his pockets were full of money.

At the inaugural parade, President Roosevelt rode in a big, black, open car followed by the army band, then followed famous First Nations chiefs and great warriors, such as Little Plume (Piegan), Buckskin Charlie (Southern Ute), Quanah Parker (Comanche), Hollow Horn Bear (Brulé Lakota), Geronimo, and American Horse (Oglala Lakota). A unit of well-dressed, well-disciplined Indian students followed them from the Carlisle School. Nobody thought to take a picture of the Carlisle School cadets, who were there to demonstrate what a good job the government was doing "civilizing" the Indians. Nobody in fact paid much attention to the other "wild" Indians. Only the president got more attention than Geronimo. The disgusted Woodworth Clum, son of the famous John Clum (see "Geronimo's Only Capture" in part 2) and member of the inaugural committee, said men threw their hats in the air and yelled, "Hooray for Geronimo," and "Public Hero Number Two!"

Bleachers had been put up along the sides of the street, and people paid money for seats with good views. They seemed to lose interest in Roosevelt and left their seats to follow Geronimo and the others for several blocks. Roosevelt is supposed to have said he never wished to hear the name Geronimo again. However, four days later Roosevelt held a meeting with the old warriors. At that meeting Geronimo made a plea for the president to

1905 photograph of First Nations war chiefs riding in Theodore Roosevelt's inauguration parade. Geronimo is in the front row, second from the right, wearing black.

PHOTO COURTESY OF NATIONAL ARCHIVES

permit him and his people to return to their homeland, a great canyon on the headwaters of the Gila River where he was born.

Geronimo said in part, "Great Father, I look to you as I look to God. When I see your face, I think I see the face of the Great Spirit. I come here to pray to you to be good to me and my people ..."

He told how he had fought to protect his homeland:

Did I fear the Great White Chief? No. He was my enemy and the enemy of my people. His people desired the country of my people. My heart was strong against him. I said he should never have my country ... I defied the Great White Chief, for in those days, I was a fool ... I ask you to think of me as I was then. I lived in the home of my people ... they trusted me. It was right that I should give them my strength and wisdom.

When the soldiers of the Great White Chief drove me and my people from our home, we went to the mountains. When they followed us, we slew all we could. We said we would not be captured. No. We starved, but we killed. I said we would never yield, for I was a fool. So I was punished, and all my people were punished with me. The white soldiers took me and made me a prisoner far from my own country.

Great Father, other Indians have homes where they can live and be happy. I and my people have no homes. The place where we are kept is bad for us . . . We are sick there and we die. White men are in the country that was my home. I pray you tell them to go away and let my people go there and be happy.

Great Father, my hands are tied as with a rope. My heart is no longer bad. I will tell my people to obey no chief but the Great White Chief. I pray you cut the ropes and make me free. Let me die in my own country as an old man who has been punished enough and is free.[1]

Roosevelt listened respectfully and answered with understanding. "I have no anger in my heart against you. I even wish it were only a question of letting you return to your country as a free man." Then he spoke of the hostility in Arizona for Geronimo and his people and the prospect of trouble if they returned. "I should have to interfere between you. There would be more war and more bloodshed . . . it is best for you to stay where you are." He promised to confer with the secretary of Indian affairs and the secretary of war "about your case, but I do not think I can hold out any hope for you. That is all I can say, Geronimo, except that I am sorry, and have no feeling against you."

In the years that followed, Geronimo must have thought about this meeting often. It is interesting to recall that when he was dying with pneumonia he repeatedly told his step-grandson, Eugene Chihuahua, and his nephew, Asa Daklugie, he regretted surrendering and wished he had died like Victorio fighting his enemies.

Geronimo's Twenty-Three Years in Captivity

During his years as a prisoner of war, Geronimo became an entrepreneur, farmed, and was shown off to the world by his keepers.[1] The trains carrying the Apaches east often stopped to let the public see the fierce warriors the army had finally "defeated." Geronimo soon discovered that people would pay good money for a souvenir button he cut from his coat. Between stops, he'd sew more buttons back on his jacket and sell those at the next stop. He also made bows and arrows for sale, which the public gobbled up, and after seeing his success, others asked him to sell their bows and arrows as well, and he did.

Geronimo's keepers showed him off in parades along with other chiefs and at expositions where the public and well-known figures could meet and pose with him for a picture—for a small nominal fee of course—and his celebrity grew. The photograph accompanying this story shows Geronimo first at Fort Sam Houston in San Antonio waiting to go to Florida, next at the Mount Vernon Barracks in Alabama, and then, after being transferred to the Fort Sill Military Reservation, being shown off at the 1904 Louisiana Purchase Exposition in St. Louis with his bow and arrows for sale, and finally on June 11, 1905, driving a Model C Locomobile at the Miller brothers' 101 Ranch, located southwest of Ponca City, Oklahoma. The photograph was taken during a special 101 Ranch show for the U.S. press. The Ponca Indian in full headdress to Geronimo's left is Edward Le Clair Sr. Geronimo so admired Le Clair's beaded vest that it was presented to him later in the day. When Geronimo died at Fort Sill in 1909 while still a prisoner of war, he was nearing ninety years old, and he was buried in the vest.

Eugene Chihuahua was a scout in the Seventh Cavalry and in uniform when he met Geronimo selling his bows and arrows on a cool winter's day outside a mercantile store in Lawton, Oklahoma, near Fort Sill. Geronimo said, "Grandson, I need some whiskey. Take this money and get some for me." The request put Eugene in a tight situation. Selling whiskey to an Indian could bring a jail term with years at hard labor. Eugene thought he had soldier friends who would buy it for him, but his uniform coat was too tight to hide it. A white friend agreed to buy him a quart and told him to get a good, fast horse. Eugene had only an army mount, but Geronimo had a fast pony.

Geronimo during his years in captivity. Top left, under guard and expecting execution in San Antonio at Fort Sam Houston, photographed by Eugene K. Sturdevant in September 1886; top right, with Chihuahua, Naiche, Loco, and Nana at Mount Vernon Barracks in Alabama, ca. 1890; bottom left, Geronimo from Fort Sill as a celebrity at the St. Louis Exposition in 1904 selling his bows and arrows; bottom right, Geronimo driving a Locomobile at the Miller brothers' 101 Ranch, located southwest of Ponca City, Oklahoma, during a press event, 1905.
PHOTOS COURTESY OF LIBRARY OF CONGRESS AND NATIONAL ARCHIVES

They swapped horses. The white friend put the bottle of whiskey on a two-by-four fence brace next to the saloon. Eugene came charging by, snatched the bottle, and hightailed it out of town. He and Geronimo rode to Cache Creek where there was some timber. They watered their horses, hobbled them on good grass, and drank the whiskey. They went to sleep with no cover but their saddle blankets.

Near morning, Eugene woke up in a cold, drizzling rain. Geronimo was coughing, and his face was hot to the touch. He told Eugene he had been sick all night. Eugene got him to the Fort Sill hospital, where the doctor said he had pneumonia. Eugene sent word to Geronimo's wife Azul, and she brought Daklugie with her to the hospital. Daklugie and Eugene took turns at twelve-hour shifts to stay with him. People came to see him, but the only ones the nurses let in were Eugene, Daklugie, and his wife. Geronimo took the doctor's medicine, and Eugene and Daklugie also made medicine (prayer and other ceremonies) for him. At times, Geronimo was delirious, but he still recognized them.

When Daklugie was born, his mother, Geronimo's sister, Ishton, had a very hard time with the birth, and his father, Juh, was away on a raid in Mexico. Geronimo made medicine on Mount Bowie for his sister, who he thought was going to die. The great Apache God, *Ussen*, spoke to him, "Go back to your sister. Both she and her child will survive. You will live to be an old man, and you will die a natural death." It was as *Ussen* said. Daklugie was born, and his mother lived. Geronimo in all his war years was sometimes badly wounded, but he didn't die.

Daklugie was with his uncle the night he died. The old warrior fighting to stay alive and awaiting the arrival of his son, Robert, and daughter, Eva, from the Indian school at Chilocco two hundred miles north, drifted in and out of consciousness. He made Daklugie promise to take his daughter Eva into his house and not let her marry. He believed that she would die in childbirth because the women of his family had great difficulty. Daklugie said, "Ramona and I will take your daughter and love her as our own. But how can I prevent her from marrying?" Geronimo said, "She will obey you. She has been taught to obey. See that she does."

He died with his fingers clutching Daklugie's hand. Robert and Eva arrived late, even for the funeral, because the military officer in charge, Lt. George A. Purington, had notified them by letter rather than by telegram that their father was passing away and they needed to come.

The government would not let the Apaches, out of respect, burn his house or bury his best warhorse. He was buried with his most treasured possessions, and Daklugie made sure that he had his best pony for his journey to the Happy Land. The Apaches guarded his grave for months. Not one of his warriors failed to volunteer to take their turn guarding the grave, and many who never rode with him on the warpath also took a turn. They did this because greedy traders and White Eyes, who had no respect for *Ussen* or the dead, had robbed many graves, and the Apaches had not forgotten that soldiers had cut off the head of Mangas Coloradas, boiled the flesh away, and sent the skull to the Smithsonian Institution.

The story goes that a few years after the grave was no longer guarded, two Apaches dug up the grave, took the skull, and sold it. They were watched for years, but they never showed any evidence of having extra money. There is also the story, strongly denied, of army officers in the Yale Skull and Bones Society taking the skull in 1918 after Daklugie and others moved to Mescalero in 1913.[2]

EARLY LIFE ON THE MESCALERO RESERVATION

For the first ten years after the creation of their reservation, the Mescalero suffered from "weak or wicked" agents who stole their rations or let contractors provide them with substandard materials. During this time, Victorio and Nana and their band of Mimbreño Apaches attempted to establish roots on the reservation with the Mescaleros. An inept agent, denying rations to Victorio, drove him off the reservation and into one of the bloodiest Apache wars southern New Mexico, Arizona, and northern Mexico ever experienced. During the Victorio War, the army, convinced the Mescaleros were supplying Victorio with arms and warriors, invaded the reservation with a thousand soldiers and three hundred Chiricahua scouts. Their objectives were to group the Mescaleros around the agency, where they could be closely watched, and to disarm and unhorse every Indian. With a few minor exceptions, the Mescaleros were innocent of the army's charges, and the injustice of what happened left the Mescaleros bitter against the bluecoats for years.

Six months after the army left the reservation in January of 1881, William Henry Harrison (W. H. H.) Llewellyn, one of the best agents to manage the reservation, arrived. Llewellyn respected the Mescaleros and their customs and religious beliefs, and they respected him. He established an Indian court and the tribal police, who brought stability to a place of chaotic situations. During Llewellyn's tenure, he had to deal with the government's attempt to establish the Jicarilla Apaches on the Mescalero Reservation, which, in the eyes of the Jicarilla and the Mescaleros, was a major mistake. Within three years, the Jicarilla had left Mescalero bound for their own reservation in the northern mountains of New Mexico.

Ten years passed after Llewellyn left, and the Mescaleros tolerated a string of mediocre agents. Agent lieutenant V. E. Stottler arrived with his policies, which included no work–no eat. Under Stottler's directives all children were to be separated from their parents at age five to attend the reservation boarding school and the men were to cut their hair Anglo style and wear Anglos clothes. Each family was to live in a log cabin, and the men were to put fences around their property for the ten sheep for every man, woman, and child Stottler planned to buy for them to live on. The women were to learn to make blankets and rugs as the Navajo did.

Stottler's requirement for all Indian children to attend boarding school was based on the belief within the Bureau of Indian Affairs that Indian culture had to be destroyed for the Indians to do well in white society and that the best way to do that was separating children from the parents and giving them a white, Christian education. Despite the white society forced on them, the Mescaleros adapted, and remnants of their culture survived.

The Mescaleros were fortunate to have strong chiefs who, beginning with Cadette in 1872 and ending with Peso in 1928, endured and helped make life better for their people through good times and bad. In 1913 the Mescaleros agreed to accept as brothers the Chiricahuas who had been prisoners of war at Fort Sill, Oklahoma. The Chiricahuas and their leaders brought increased vitality to reservation life through their experience in raising cattle, dealing every day with the whites, learning to live in houses, and making use of modern inventions to enhance their lives.

The Chiricahuas and Mimbreños had well-known leaders, including Geronimo, Juh, Naiche, Chihuahua, Loco, and Nana, who led them toward living well in the Anglo world during their time in captivity. When the Chiricahuas came to Mescalero, one of their main leaders and spokesmen was Asa Daklugie, son of Juh, nephew of Geronimo. Daklugie had spent eight years at the Carlisle Indian School and had studied animal husbandry. He helped establish the Chiricahuas on the Mescalero Reservation and ensured their success.

The tribal police earned respect and wide praise from white ranchers and law officers when, in the dead of winter in early 1908, they tracked and killed the Mescalero, Kedinchin, who had killed a young white man, Don McLane. Don McLane was the last white man killed by a Mescalero on the reservation.

The Mescaleros Penned Up at Bosque Redondo

EARLY IN 1862, GEN. JAMES HENRY CARLTON, COMMANDER OF THE CALIFORNIA VOL-unteers, marched east to fight the Confederate army in New Mexico. After a major battle with warriors under Cochise and Mangas Coloradas at Apache Pass, his advanced scouts reached the Río Grande in July 1862. There General Carlton learned the Confederate army no longer existed in New Mexico. Most of the Confederates had packed up and gone back to Texas and San Antonio. New Mexico was in a bad way. It had been the scene of battles between Union and Confederate forces; it suffered almost continuous raids by angry Indians; and, without law and order, it was in chaos. General Carlton took over and for the next four years was the absolute ruler of New Mexico.

Quartermaster stores area at Bosque Redondo, ca. 1866
PHOTO COURTESY OF LYNDA SÁNCHEZ/EVE BALL COLLECTION

It soon became apparent to Carlton that his biggest challenge in controlling the country was to keep his soldiers busy, and that the best way to do that was to put the Indians in their place on tightly controlled reservations. With the help of Governor Connelly, he cajoled his old friend, a highly reluctant Kit Carson, into taking command of troops in the field fighting the Indians and to spearhead the attacks with New Mexico militiamen.

Carlton's first order to Kit Carson, dated September 27, 1862, was to reoccupy Fort Stanton on the Bonito River. While on his way to Fort Stanton, Carson received additional instructions that read in part, ". . . All Indian men of that tribe [Mescalero] are to be killed whenever and wherever you can find them. The women and children will not be harmed, but you will take them prisoner and feed them at Fort Stanton . . . If the Indians send in a flag and desire to treat for peace, say to the bearer . . . [that] you have been sent to punish them for their treachery and their crimes; that you have no power to make peace; that you are there to kill them; that if they beg for peace, their chiefs and twenty of their principal men must come to Santa Fe and have a talk there."

Kit Carson was appalled by the order, but as a sworn military officer could do nothing but follow it. The Mescaleros living around Sierra Blanca and El Capitan in the Sacramento Mountains, peaceful, not raiding, and asking for a truce, were shocked at the attack by soldiers directed by the savagery of Carlton's orders.

Early in November of 1862, Maj. William McLeave with two companies of Californians managed to get within range of five hundred Mescaleros camped at the mouth of Dog Canyon without being discovered. His attack drove the surprised Indians up the canyon and into the Sacramentos, where they decided to hike over the mountains and put themselves under the protection of Kit Carson. Arriving at Fort Stanton they put Carson, under orders to kill the men without mercy, in an awkward position, and the Apaches knew it, but his conscience forbade him to fire into a band of frightened people asking for mercy.

In November, Carson sent five leading Mescaleros accompanied by a military escort and their agent, Lorenzo Labadie, to Santa Fe for talks with Carlton. Chief Cadette was their spokesman. There were no negotiations in Santa Fe. Carlton had already made up his mind to pen up the Mescaleros on a large loop of land formed by the Pecos River and covered in cottonwood trees in east-central New Mexico. It was a favorite camping place for Apaches known as Bosque Redondo (Round Grove). Carlton had already directed that a new military post, Fort Sumner, be built nearby. The Apaches didn't want to go into captivity, and ranchers running cattle along the Pecos didn't want them there, but Carlton's word was law. By the beginning of March 1863, more than four hundred Mescalero men, women, and children had surrendered and moved to General Carlton's "reservation" at Bosque Redondo. They had come in the few wagons Carson could spare or walked carrying their belongings on their shoulders and were drawing rations at Fort Sumner.

Carlton's grand vision of taming the Mescaleros depended on teaching them to farm and to follow the "superior" ways of the Americans. By mid-summer 1863, the

Mescaleros had developed fields to grow crops and had living quarters that would suffice and get them by.

During the summer of 1863, General Carlton sent Kit Carson and his militia north to subdue the Navajos. Carson was successful and took many prisoners. General Carlton ordered Carson to send the Navajo prisoners of war south to Bosque Redondo. It was a 450-mile trail of suffering the Navajos named "The Long Walk." Navajos and Mescalero Apaches, both speaking Athabasca dialects, didn't get along and fought like two brothers quarreling over a woman. Carlton had told the Apaches that Bosque Redondo was their land, their reservation, and it was probably large enough to support them, but not both Apaches and sixteen times their number in Navajos. When Carson had fully conquered the Navajos, over nine thousand had traveled the Long Walk to Bosque Redondo, but many died along the way.[1]

Five Hundred Mescaleros Disappear
Overnight from Bosque Redondo

The Mescalero Apaches penned up at Bosque Redondo on the Pecos River were bitter. General Carlton had told them Bosque Redondo was theirs, not land they had to share with the hated Navajos. With the arrival of the Navajos, the Apaches had to share and often give away the fruits of all their labor of laying out and planting fields, digging irrigation canals, and trying to grow a crop. The Apaches had a successful crop in 1863, but after the Navajos arrived nothing again came to fruition. Every year there was a new disaster. Worms, blight, boring insects, drought, floods, frost, and hail

Seven years after disappearing from Bosque Redondo, Cadette led his people to the new Mescalero Reservation near the great sacred mountain, Sierra Blanca.
PHOTO PETE LINDSLEY, COURTESY OF THE LYNDA SÁNCHEZ COLLECTION

all took their toll on the Mescaleros' work to keep from starving in the winter, the Season of the Ghost Face. After the Mescaleros left, the Navajos believed the land was cursed and refused to plant any more crops.

Living conditions in the camps of the Mescaleros and Navajos were an outrage. They lived in hovels made from materials they had brought with them or that had been doled out by the soldiers, and when the winter winds blew in off the prairie, they suffered from the cold. They had to wear worn-out and ragged clothes, and as their rags fell to pieces, they had to go nearly naked. The water from the Pecos had high alkali content, and its bitterness made them sick. Sanitary facilities were nonexistent. The demand for firewood or anything to burn had turned the once green bosque into a barren dust bowl. Women had to walk or take wagons, sometimes as far as eighteen miles, out on the llano (dry prairie) to dig mesquite roots for firewood. By 1865 the Indian agent Lorenzo Labadie reported that the Indians were being fed cattle that had died of disease. Even when there was no meat, they weren't allowed to hunt off the "reservation" or to find mescal to cook and save for lean winter times.

As the bad times spiraled into 1865, it became clear to the Apaches that it would be better to die free and on the run than to starve to death while their children picked through horse apples looking for undigested grain for their mothers' cook pots. Several times, Chief Cadette told General Carlton and Captain Updegraff, commander at Fort Sumner, that the Apaches had to have their own reservation; they could not stay at Bosque Redondo. Captain Updegraff believed Cadette, but there was little he could do. Late in the summer of 1865, the Apaches at Bosque Redondo began making plans to leave.

The summer of 1865 was a disaster for Bosque Redondo crops planted by the Mescaleros. Frost appeared later than normal and destroyed a first planting. Later in the summer, hail fell from angry, black clouds and beat growing plants to pieces. Blight and insects destroyed the crops that survived frost and hail and suffered through drought and short water in the irrigation canals. With an extra eight thousand Navajo mouths to feed, the once adequate rations set aside for the Apaches disappeared into hungry bellies much faster than expected, and with the war back east ending with the South starving and on its knees, few supplies made it west, and virtually none were sent to Indians imprisoned at Bosque Redondo. General Carlton ordered rations reduced to half a pound of bread and four ounces of meat per person or three-quarters of a pound of solid food per day.

As summer drifted into fall, Carlton had to reduce rations again. Weakened warriors felt their strength drain away and watched as their families became increasingly gaunt, dying from starvation, disease, and bad water. Many planned to break out, but the chiefs told them to wait. They had a plan. Their argument was that if the warriors left a few at a time, they would be followed and killed or made to come back. If the entire tribe left at one time, like a flock of birds scattering from a bush in all directions, a few might be caught, but most would get away.

In councils unknown to the White Eye civilians and bluecoat soldiers, and with details unknown to this day, warriors and chiefs developed their plan and made ready to leave under the watchful eyes of their keepers. During the night of November 3, 1865, every Apache who could travel, nearly five hundred, disappeared from Bosque Redondo, leaving behind only nine too sick to move, and a few days later these were gone too. They scattered in all directions, some east to the plains to join with Comanches, some south to join their brothers in the Guadalupe and Davis Mountains in Texas, some west toward the Sacramento Mountains to join Santana's band, and some beyond the Río Grande into the western mountains of New Mexico and Arizona. No one knows for sure where all the Mescaleros went.

When the Mescaleros left, it was already cold, and they had no supplies. Winter was coming, and while a few bluecoat patrols were sent out to look for them, it was impossible to chase an entire tribe, and if truth be known, it is likely Carlton was more relieved than angry they had left, probably thinking the winter would do what the army would not, and that there were five hundred fewer mouths to feed with fast-vanishing supplies.

Seven years later, when the reality of a Mescalero reservation in the Sacramento Mountains began to emerge in 1872, the Mescaleros began ending their diaspora from Bosque Redondo, and by 1875–1876, most had entered their own reservation in the mountains where hunting was good and water was sweet.[1]

Victorio on the Mescalero Reservation

VICTORIO WAS ON THE MESCALERO RESERVATION LESS THAN THREE MONTHS BEFORE he left to start a war with the White Eyes and Mexicans that lasted over a year, spilled much blood, destroyed property, and had significant portions of both the U.S. and Mexican armies as well as civilian militias chasing him on both sides of the border.[1]

Victorio, chief of the Mimbreño Apaches, accepted living on a reservation at Ojo Caliente around 1870, two years before Cochise settled on his reservation. The Mimbreños were content at Ojo Caliente, but they were moved to the Tularosa Reservation, about seventy miles northwest of Ojo Caliente, in 1872. Two years later the Tularosa Reservation was closed, and they were moved back to Ojo Caliente in 1874. Three years later, April/May 1877, the Bureau of Indian Affairs under the Department of Interior decided on a policy of reservation consolidation and had John Clum, who had been sent to Ojo Caliente to arrest Geronimo, move the Mimbreños to San Carlos when he returned with Geronimo in shackles bound for the San Carlos guardhouse.

Lieutenant Britton Davis aptly called San Carlos a hellhole. It was a place of insufferable heat, dust, snakes, and mosquitoes with their diseases. After less than four months at San Carlos, Victorio had enough and broke out in September 1877 with about three hundred Mimbreños. In late fall of that year, after losing more than fifty dead in the chase by the army and their Apache scouts, nearly two hundred Mimbreños, sans Victorio, surrendered to the army at Fort Wingate and were promptly relocated to Ojo Caliente. Victorio soon reappeared, and General Hatch promised he would do what he could to keep them there if they stayed on their best behavior, and they did, while Department of Interior bureaucrats tried to decide what to do with them. In August 1878, with the army pushing the Department of Interior to do something, the decision was made to return the Mimbreños to San Carlos. Enraged at the pusillanimous, face-saving (the bureaucrats didn't want it to seem that the Indians forced them to do anything) decision, Victorio and more than eighty followers, mostly warriors, took off. In an unusually wet fall, even Apache scouts couldn't find Victorio and his followers, which led the Bureau of Indian Affairs to move the remaining 170 Mimbreños, under tight guard, back to San Carlos in December

Apache Medicine Song, by Fredrick Remington, ca. 1908, suggests how Victorio and his warriors were making medicine to recruit Mescalero warriors the night before he left the reservation.
COURTESY OF SID RICHARDSON MUSEUM, FORT WORTH, TEXAS

1878. That same month, Nana, Victorio's segundo (number two), with sixty-three old men, women, and children, showed up at the Mescalero Reservation and asked to be taken in. The agent, Fred C. Godfroy, who was taking cuts of Apache rations and supplies for his own benefit, was happy to have them and let them camp in the Rinconada. However, a number of young warriors with Nana came in separately over the mountains and weren't in Godfroy's count. This allowed them to come and go as they pleased or when Nana wanted to use them to keep Victorio informed of what was happening at the reservation.

In February of 1879, Victorio and his men appeared at Ojo Caliente. Victorio begged the officer in charge to let them go anywhere except San Carlos. In April, word came that the Mimbreños would be sent to Mescalero. On hearing this, Victorio thought better of his earlier plea and took off again.

In the spring of 1879, Nana, wise to Godfroy's theft of Mescalero rations and supplies, had a few of his warriors waylay a wagonload of stolen rations Godfroy was shipping to a warehouse in Las Cruces. Nana cached part of the rations for his future use and gave the rest to the Mescaleros since it was theirs anyway. When word got out of what had happened, the whites, fearful that stealing their rations would send the Mescaleros on a rampage, were outraged at Godfroy, who was soon replaced by timid, by-the-book S. A. Russell, who had a long, white beard that reached to his waist, of which he was very proud.

When Victorio reappeared at Mescalero in June with thirteen of his warriors, he told Russell he wanted to settle there and asked for rations. Russell told him that required permission from Washington, which took about three weeks. Victorio waited, but, as the days passed, he began to be suspicious that Russell was setting him up for some kind of confrontation. July slipped into August, and still no rations were offered. Growing hungrier and more belligerent by the day, Victorio and his men spread rumors that they were thinking about seizing government stores and going on the warpath.

Victorio, camped in the Rinconada with Nana's group, met with large groups of Mescalero warriors and told them they needed to leave with him if he broke out of the reservation. Mescalero chief San Juan led Victorio and his men to Dr. Joe Blazer, who ran a sawmill and a supply store on the reservation. San Juan explained the situation, and Blazer, hoping to set the Mimbreños at ease until Russell's request was approved, gave them from his own supplies a fat steer, flour, sugar, and coffee. A quiet week passed until someone showed up with a supply of *tiswin*. There was a big drunk, and as often happened at these "parties," an argument developed, and a Mescalero was killed. The Mimbreños were blamed for both the *tiswin* and the killing.

To add to the turmoil, about this time a group of men from Silver City appeared on the reservation. Among them was a judge from Mesilla, no less than the famous colonel Albert Fountain, and the prosecuting attorney for Grant County, where a grand jury had issued an indictment against Victorio for horse theft and murder. Knowing about the warrant and recognizing the men, who actually were on a hunting trip, Victorio grew increasingly nervous.

Saturday was ration day at Mescalero. Victorio and his people came and stood in line for their allotment, but when their turn came, they were told they would have to wait. After coming back several times and getting the same answer, Victorio was convinced he was being set up for capture and to be turned over to the men in the hunting party. He went to Russell and demanded to know what was going on. When it appeared Russell wasn't giving him a straight answer, Victorio grabbed him by his beard and dragged him around the room, stopping occasionally to give him a kick. Russell begged his interpreter, José Carillo, "Speak pretty to them," but Carillo, realizing it was useless to try to reason with Victorio, tried to make Russell understand that hunger was an immediate problem.

Victorio, realizing bullying Russell was doing no good, let go after giving him a final kick, much to the enjoyment of his warriors. They went down to the mill, where Dr. Blazer again gave them beef, flour, sugar, and coffee. They went back to their camp for the night in a little canyon in back of the mill but out of sight of the agency. Restless Mescalero warriors, anxious for one more raid off the reservation, came in small groups to visit with Victorio and left smiling.

In the meantime, Russell, scared to death that Victorio might kill him or start an uprising, wired Fort Stanton to send troops for protection. A company of cavalry was dispatched with all speed. As the soldiers approached the mill, a bugle sounded, and Victorio and his men heard it. Victorio went down to Blazer's mill and shook his hand. He said he was afraid to stay any longer, and he is said to have told Blazer, "My friend, this my last day. Going back to my country."

Within minutes, Victorio and his warriors were gone, and along with him were many Mescaleros, including Running Water, Manchito, Caje, and Muchacho Negro.[2] As many as three hundred bored and restless Mescaleros, including those living in the Davis Mountains and the reservation, as well as Lipan Apaches, Comanches, and Navajos, eventually joined Victorio in his year of war with the White Eyes and Mexicans.

Invasion of the Mescalero Reservation

IN THE FALL OF 1879, VICTORIO, CHIEF OF THE MIMBREÑO APACHES, WAS SPOOKED INTO leaving the Mescalero Reservation, where he had agreed to stay with his people. It was the start of the Victorio War. He raided in the Arizona mountains to the west, came back east across Chihuahua and into New Mexico, and then disappeared to winter somewhere south in Mexico. In January of 1880, Victorio was found in a canyon on the upper Rio Puerco in the New Mexico Black Range. There he had a two-day battle with army troops

A Cavalryman's Breakfast on the Plains, by Fredrick Remington, ca. 1892, suggests the force the Mescaleros faced in the middle of their reservation on April 16, 1880, when they were invaded by more than one thousand cavalry troopers and three hundred Apache scouts. The original painting now hangs at the Amon Carter Museum in Fort Worth, Texas.
COURTESY OF FINE ART/ALAMY

under Major Morrow before he disappeared, only to reappear in another battle with Major Morrow in a San Andres Mountains canyon on the south side of the Jornada del Muerto near Aleman's Well before disappearing once more.

The entire time these fights and raids were taking place, the Mescaleros were minding their business on their reservation in the Sacramento Mountains of central New Mexico. Although there was no proof, the army believed the Mescaleros had to be supplying Victorio with guns, bullets, horses, and warriors. In January of 1880, Colonel Hatch, with a few other officers, began developing a highly secret plan to invade the Mescalero Reservation, take all their arms and horses, and keep them penned up close to the agency until Victorio was brought to heel or killed. It is true that some supply of Victorio from the reservation happened, but it was not nearly of the magnitude the army thought and didn't justify an invasion.

On April 16, 1880, a thousand U.S. soldiers and more than three hundred Indian scouts from forts all over the Southwest and Texas converged from different directions on the Mescalero agency headquarters, all appearing within an hour of high noon. Colonel Hatch had told Agent Russell to order the Mescaleros to come into the agency with their horses and firearms. Russell had no idea the army planned to disarm the Mescaleros since they needed their rifles to hunt. When the soldiers appeared and the Mescaleros saw what was happening, some tried to run and were shot down. Even so, some Mescaleros who had not come to the agency managed to escape and left the reservation for the Apache camps in the Sierra Madre.

The army collected all the Mescalero ponies, more than two hundred, in a stonewall corral and then drove the herd over the mountains for safekeeping at Fort Stanton. Hatch promised that when Victorio surrendered the Mescalero ponies would be returned. The Mescaleros got back forty-one of the horses taken. With their horses gone, Colonel Hatch made the Mescaleros live in the stonewall corral, which already had three to five inches of dry manure under the two days of fresh manure from all the ponies that had just been there. The Apaches soon became so sick Colonel Hatch had to let them camp outside the corral, but in plain sight of soldiers camped around the agency. By September, Hatch had widened the area over which the Apaches could camp but still kept a tight hold on their movements.

In October of 1880, a Mexican army contingent under Gen. Joaquin Terrazas found Victorio, running low on ammunition, camped in the Tres Castillos Mountains in Chihuahua. He wiped out Victorio, but Victorio's segundo, his second in command, old Nana, who with a few warriors had been sent to look for more ammunition and hunt, escaped.

In January 1881, nine months after the invasion, the army was ordered off the Mescalero Reservation. In the middle of the twentieth century, old Mescaleros were still outraged and bitter about their inhumane treatment by the army on their own reservation.

Agent W. H. H. Llewellyn, Tata Crooked Nose

Most of the early Mescalero Reservation Indian agents were, in the words of C. L. Sonnichsen, "weak or wicked." However, one of the best agents, William Henry Harrison Llewellyn, started work on June 16, 1881. He had recently come to the Southwest from Nebraska, and fortunately he had his own constructive ideas about Indian management. He was polite, considered their welfare, and didn't hesitate to apply discipline when the Mescaleros deserved it. The Mescaleros respected him and gave him the name "Tata Crooked Nose," because of his prominent nose with a Roman hook.

From the moment Llewellyn arrived at the agency, he had his hands full. The night he arrived, the Mescaleros burned a witch. Llewellyn's wife, arriving about a month later, just

Mescalero Apache agency in 1881 looking southeast down Tularosa Canyon about the time W. H. H. Llewellyn arrived
PHOTO COURTESY OF NEW MEXICO STATE UNIVERSITY LIBRARY, ARCHIVES AND SPECIAL COLLECTIONS

missed Nana's warriors who had destroyed a Mexican family in their wagon as they passed White Sands. Then, soon after he arrived, an Apache family came to him with newborn twins. The Apaches believed twins were not natural and that one had to be destroyed. He was asked to choose which one had to die. Neither child was destroyed, nor was Llewellyn asked to make such a decision again.

Llewellyn soon organized a Mescalero police force of fifteen Mescaleros and placed them under the command of Thomas Branigan from Las Cruces. In those days, because the reservations were managed by the army, the agent had the title of major, and the chief of police, captain. Captain Branigan took over the police force Llewellyn had begun and shaped it into a competent and respected force that did much to stabilize reservation society.

Llewellyn gave the Apaches direction in work that needed to be done. He detailed some as herders to watch their livestock and others to prepare land for cultivation. When he arrived, there were sixty-six acres under cultivation. In his first year, he added an additional fifty acres. The following year, he had an additional seventy acres under cultivation. He added a doctor to the agency staff, and increased the school year for Mescalero children. Instead of five months per year, school went in session for a full term to give the Mescalero children full benefit of the teachers who were there and to give them as much opportunity for education as the reservation could provide. The first Mescalero children went to the Indian boarding school in Albuquerque, and he had two log houses built as a start toward better housing. Unlike Stottler, who appeared fifteen years after his arrival, Llewellyn was not a martinet. He never applied overbearing, preemptory force to make the Mescaleros adopt the ways of the *Indah* (White men).

In 1882 faraway Washington bureaucrats decided to move the Jicarilla Apaches from their own reservation in the mountains of northern New Mexico to the Mescalero Reservation (see chapter 6, part 7). In July of 1883, Llewellyn began supervising the transfer of the Jicarillas over five hundred miles south to three camps on the reservation. It took forty-seven days on the road. On the way, smallpox broke out, and six people died.

The Jicarillas were not happy. They believed that their god had told them that if they left their northern mountains they would surely die. The Mescaleros weren't happy because they felt the Jicarillas were crowding them off their land and overhunting the wild game. There were 462 Mescaleros and 721 Jicarillas. The Jicarillas thought they should have some of their men on the Indian police force. Branigan said no. The force had to work as a coherent whole, and he knew that, at least in their early years on the reservation, the Jicarillas wouldn't take orders from Mescaleros or vice versa.

Llewellyn tried to do his best for all the Apaches. For example, he bought five hundred head of cattle, divided them between the Mescaleros and Jicarillas, took out a membership for them in the Lincoln County Cattle Growers Association, and sat back to watch the herds grow. He soon discovered that, unlike a valuable horse, the Apaches treated cows as just food on the hoof and the herds slowly evaporated.

By 1885, the Jicarillas began leaving Mescalero and heading north. The army, busy with Geronimo, left them alone because they weren't bothering anyone. They made a camp outside of Santa Fe where they eventually convinced the governor to give them land in the mountains where they wanted to live.

W. H. H. Llewellyn, a staunch Republican, resigned his position as Indian agent late in 1884 after Democrat Grover Cleveland was elected president. Tom Branigan stayed on as chief of tribal police until the newly appointed agent, Fletcher J. Cowart, arrived on November 18, 1885.

The Jicarilla Come to Mescalero

THE JICARILLA APACHES WHO HUNTED BUFFALO AND MADE WAR ON THE PLAINS WERE like plains tribes in the way they dressed and lived using tipis, parfleches, bow cases and quivers, and travois, a type of A-frame sledge pulled by a horse to carry goods. However, their primary camps were located in the mountains of northeastern New Mexico and southern Colorado, and they considered the mountains their home. Regardless of heavy influences of plains and pueblo cultures, the Jicarilla were Apaches with beliefs, assumptions, and behaviors in common with all who called themselves Apaches. By 1775 the more numerous Comanche had driven the Jicarilla from the plains, where they then only briefly appeared to hunt buffalo.

After nearly a hundred years of warfare, broken government promises, and near starvation, the government, between 1872 and 1874, selected a reservation for the Jicarilla around Tierra Amarilla in north-central New Mexico, about twenty-five miles from the Colorado border, for the "absolute and undisturbed occupation by the Jicarilla Apache." They were to be managed by the Southern Ute agency and receive financial subsidies, provisions, protection, land allotments, and schools. Cheated by contractors, the Jicarilla got only about half the rations paid for by the government. Rather than starve, they continued to roam and raid and get drunk on bootleg whiskey. In 1876 the Tierra Amarilla agency was designated public domain and turned over to settlers with the excuse that there was no money to pay an agent. An effort was made, but failed, to move the Jicarilla to Fort Stanton, New Mexico, next to the Mescalero Reservation.

After much political wrangling and pressure from settlers in northern New Mexico, the decision was made in 1882 to move the Jicarilla from the Tierra Amarilla and Dulce areas in northern New Mexico to the Mescalero Reservation, then managed by Major W. H. H. Llewellyn and his chief of tribal police, Capt. Thomas Branigan.[1]

In August of 1883, Llewellyn led the Jicarilla from Amargo near Dulce in northern New Mexico to Mescalero. It took forty-seven days for the Jicarillas to cover the five-hundred-plus miles between the two agencies. Six died on the road when smallpox broke

1898 colorized photograph by William Henry Jackson of Jicarilla chief James Garfield Velarde wearing presidential peace medal

PHOTO COURTESY OF NATIONAL ARCHIVES

out, a fact Llewellyn neglected to tell the Mescaleros, worried that acceptance of the Jicarilla would only get worse.

By early October 1883, there were 462 Mescaleros and 721 Jicarillas on the Mescalero reservation. Llewellyn settled the Jicarilla in three camps, one on Río Tularosa, one at Three Rivers, and one on Carrizo Creek, and he did the best he could for all the Apaches under his charge. When the boarding school at Mescalero filled up, he built another at Three Rivers. He bought five hundred head of cattle and divided them between the Jicarilla and Mescaleros and registered the reservation with the Lincoln County Cattle Growers Association, expecting the herd to increase. However, he soon learned that to an Apache a horse was valuable property (the Mescaleros had about five hundred, the Jicarilla about a thousand), but cattle were just food on the hoof that were soon gambled away and quickly converted to beef.

Neither the Jicarilla nor Mescalero were happy with reservation arrangements. Captain Branigan allowed only Mescaleros to be tribal police. He had to be sure that his officers got along with each other and could depend on their fellows in tight situations. The Jicarilla considered Branigan's police policy eminently unfair since there were nearly half again as many Jicarilla as there were Mescaleros. On the other hand, the Mescaleros, who were careful not to overhunt their land, saw the Jicarilla, more numerous than the Mescaleros and used to plentiful game from the Rockies in northern New Mexico, within three years hunting and trapping the reservation's once plentiful game until it was scarce and hard to find. There were often fights between members of the two bands over games of chance, the Mescaleros, being experienced players when it came to monte and other games, often took the Jicarillas for every penny they had, although each side accused the other of cheating.

In late 1884, Llewellyn left as agent, and Fletcher J. Cowart arrived in November of 1885. By the time Cowart arrived, Jicarillas had been leaving in small groups to return north. On their way, they didn't bother anyone and purposefully stayed out of the way of White Eyes. Cowart tried to get the cavalry to bring them back to Mescalero, but the army under General Miles had its hands full trying to keep Geronimo in check and refused to bother with them.

In the fall of 1886, while the government was trying to decide what to do with Geronimo, who had surrendered in September, and the Chiricahuas and Mimbreños General Miles had forced to leave San Carlos, two hundred Jicarilla left the reservation en masse, walked up the Río Grande, and made a camp outside of Santa Fe. They refused to leave until the governor listened to their grievances. Having two hundred Apaches camped on their doorstep demanding satisfaction so alarmed the citizens of the territory's cultural and legislative capital that, on February 11, 1887, the New Mexico governor issued an executive order to set aside a reservation in the Tierra Amarilla region.

The formation of the reservation was complicated by the fact that settlers who had claimed land under the Homestead Act didn't want to leave. The government began buying back the land from the settlers in 1887 in an exercise that was to take fifty years to complete. In May 1887 the remaining Jicarilla at Mescalero and Fort Stanton were returned north to unite with their brothers on their own permanent reservation. In 1901 the size of the Jicarilla Reservation was 415,713 acres, with fifteen thousand fenced acres, and they had a population of about 850.

During this time, a major chief for the Jicarilla was James Garfield Velarde. It is believed that Chief Garfield was born around 1850 and that he was about 108 when he passed away in the middle of the twentieth century.

Agent V. E. Stottler, Tata Loco

IN THE YEARS FOLLOWING ESTABLISHMENT OF THE RESERVATION IN 1873, THE MES-caleros suffered through a string of agents who badly managed supplies, often accepting goods of the worst quality that were paid for by the government at premium quality prices and letting the sutler store agents (sutler stores were army-sponsored trading posts) claim large numbers of Indians that never existed. Little, if any, work was available for Mescalero men, except farming, which they refused to do because they believed it was work for women.

As chapter 5 in part 7 discusses, William Henry Harrison Llewellyn, Tata Crooked Nose, one of the best advocates for the Mescaleros, became the Indian agent in June 1881. Polite, looking after their welfare, claiming their religious practices were as good as any white man's, hunting with them, and insisting that they follow agency rules and laws, he won their respect.

When Llewellyn left the agency, agents who followed him made slow progress, and while not liked, were tolerated. Ten years after Llewellyn left, Lt. V. E. Stottler, who didn't have the concerns or appreciation of Tata Crooked Nose for Mescalero customs, arrived determined to make the Mescaleros over into the image of the white settlers.

After his first full year as the Indian agent at Mescalero, Stottler wrote in *New Out-look*: "The Apache is a thorn in our side. Ignorant, cruel, superstitious, cunning, filthy, lazy, stubborn, treacherous, immoral, intemperate, mendacious, and an inveterate beggar besides, what greater combination of vices could one imagine [standing in opposition] to civilization and self-support? To the foregoing add twenty years of maintenance in idleness by the gratuitous issue of rations and clothing on the part of a too generous Government, and a determination on the part of the Apache to maintain the status quo at all hazards, and the outlook for a would-be Moses was simply appalling . . . I adopted the motto, 'No work, no rations,' and, with the intention of lavishly using force or pressure started in to accomplish something . . . An Indian is deficient in reasoning faculty, due, I presume, to his bump of stubbornness being so highly developed. Hence he must be

Mescalero agent Lt. V. E. Stottler with one of his charges in 1898. Cabins in the background are ones he forced the Mescaleros to build.

PHOTO COURTESY OF DENVER PUBLIC LIBRARY WESTERN HISTORY COLLECTION

treated more or less as a machine, which, once in motion, must be kept on the move by the Agent, who does all his thinking for him."[1]

Using his "force or pressure" approach, Stottler required every "adult Indian" to work six days on a two-mile, four-foot-wide ditch to bring water to the agency school farm. He directed every male Indian to select a piece of land and fence it or have his and all his relations' rations cut off until completed. Digging postholes with knives and sticks, the men put up fourteen miles of fence in six months. After they fenced the land, Stottler directed that logs be cut and hauled to the sawmill for roof and floor lumber of cabins to be built and lived in on the property. Stottler directed every male Apache to cut his hair and wear "civilized attire" under penalty of jail at hard labor if they did not. He required every Apache child to go to school, and if the parents or maternal grandmother resisted, supplies were denied, and the grandmother was put in jail, her rations cut off until she, too, agreed the child must go to school. In an effort to eradicate Mescalero culture, he forbade tribal dances and ceremonies. He brought in Navajo weavers to teach the women how to card, spin, and dye wool and weave blankets, using wool from five thousand head of sheep (ten for every man, woman, and child) he purchased for the Mescaleros. He intended to eliminate all rations except beef and clothing within two years and all beef within another two years. He claimed the entire elimination of *tiswin* production and public drunkenness.

Lieutenant Stottler believed he had forced the Mescaleros into "a prosperous future and independent self-support," that eventually the reservation boundary would no longer exist, and that they would be absorbed into white culture. But, as soon as he retired in June of 1898, the Mescaleros began, with few exceptions, to return to their old ways, some still living in tipis, at least in the summer, as late as 1950. No known examples of Mescalero blanket weaving exist, and only a few of Mescaleros own sheep.

"Kill the Indian . . . Save the Man"

AMONG THE MANY PROBLEMS AND ADJUSTMENTS TO RESERVATION LIFE ENDURED BY THE Apaches, or all Indian tribes for that matter, was the preservation of their culture. Few Indian agents were as blatant about destroying First Nations culture as Lt. V. E. Stottler was for the Mescaleros, discussed in the chapter above. Well-meaning people and the federal bureaucracy believed that American-European culture and religion were clearly superior to that of the First Nations people (by comparison they believed the Indians didn't have any culture and their religious beliefs were pure superstition, providing no moral guidance). Therefore, for the Indian to survive in the Anglo world, Indian culture and religion had to

Boys at the Jicarilla boarding school ca. 1910. Note the military-style uniforms and nearly identical Anglo-style haircuts.
PHOTO COURTESY OF NEW MEXICO STATE UNIVERSITY LIBRARY, ARCHIVES AND SPECIAL COLLECTIONS

go. Stottler instituted a no-work, no-eat policy, forbade ceremonies and dances, and tried to make the Mescaleros start little fenced-in ranches and live in log cabins instead of tipis.

One of Stottler's proudest metrics of success was the forcing of every Indian child on the reservation between the ages of five and eighteen to attend the reservation boarding school. He and the rest of the bureaucracy believed that the surest method for destroying Indian culture was separating the child from its parents and then providing the child an education in Anglo language, beliefs, and manual skills and some ability to read, write, and do simple arithmetic. The model for educating Indian children came from Richard Henry Pratt, an army officer who retired on the brigadier general's list in 1904. Pratt established the Carlisle Indian Industrial School at Carlisle, Pennsylvania, in 1879. By 1900, virtually every Indian boarding school in the United States used Pratt's educational approach.

In the last years of Pratt's career, he became embroiled in a major dispute with the Bureau of Indian Affairs and was forced into retirement in 1904. Nevertheless, Pratt's model for compulsory education was used not only for Indians, but for African Americans, Puerto Ricans, Latinos, Pacific Islanders, Asian Americans, and Mormons. Some have called Pratt's forced cultural destruction "cultural genocide." However, as wrong-headed as his and other ideas of the late nineteenth century appear now, Pratt believed that Indians needed to claim their rightful place as American citizens. To do this, he believed Indians needed to renounce their tribal way of life, convert to Christianity, abandon their reservations, and find education and employment among the "best classes" of Americans, or as he was often quoted as saying, "kill the Indian . . . to save the man," in rebuttal to General Sheridan's comment, "The only good Indian is a dead Indian."

The Pratt model for destroying Indian culture required that an Indian child be separated from its parents at five or six years of age and continuously kept in school until about age eighteen. The child was given an English name, had its hair cut short Anglo style, and was made to wear a uniform. They were forced never to speak, even to each other, in the native language of their parents, and if they failed to speak English or violated other rules, they received martial punishment. They were subject to strict military protocols that marched them in columns everywhere, and they had to follow signals (e.g., a ringing bell) for when to sit down, to stand up, to begin eating, etc. They were sent to church or chapel regularly and were expected to become Christians. They followed a "Uniform Course of Study," which meant they were taught to read, write, and do elementary arithmetic, but mostly underwent vocational training for boys and domestic training for girls. In the summers the students at Carlisle were sent to live and work on Dutch farms around Carlisle to learn farming from the farmers. Especially bright students at other reservation boarding schools might be sent on to the school at Chilocco, Oklahoma, or even to the Carlisle Industrial School in Pennsylvania started by Pratt. Unfortunately, the death rate for Indian boarding-school students was about three times that of the general population. Tragically, for example, one of Geronimo's sons, the bright, twenty-two-year-old Chappo sent off to the Carlisle School, returned six years later with tuberculosis and died at Mount Vernon Barracks.

THE CHIEFS OF THE MESCALEROS

In the days before the arrival of General Carlton and the California column in 1862, the Mescaleros were widely scattered. Bands under Cadette and his brothers Roman and Santana (who initially accepted the reservation area) lived mainly in the Sacramento Mountains. Another group under Juan Gómez lived in the Davis Mountains in west Texas. Still others, under a chief named Cha, lived in the Guadalupe Mountains on the New Mexico–Texas border, about one hundred miles east of El Paso. From about 1872 the Mescaleros on their reservation in the Sacramento Mountains anchored on the north end by the great sacred mountain, Sierra Blanca, accepted other Mescaleros and Lipan Apaches driven from the plains by the Comanche, Jicarilla Apaches driven from their reservation in the northern mountains of New Mexico by bureaucrats and white settlers, and Chiricahuas released from prisoner of war captivity at Fort Sill. Most of the Apaches who came to the reservation from other bands stayed. However, the Jicarilla, believing they would die out if they did not return to their northern mountains, left after a two- or three-year stay (all departures were not at the same time). This part provides glimpses into the life stories of the chiefs and their bands that came to stay at Mescalero.

Cadette

THE GREAT CHIEF OF THE MESCALEROS, BARRANQUITO, DIED IN 1857. HE LEFT BEHIND three sons or nephews (Apache kinship assumes all cousins are brothers): Santana, Cadette, and Roman. They became Mescalero leaders and were the three most important leaders around 1870 when the Mescalero reservation negotiations began. At the time of Barranquito's passing, American records mention Cadette, who had the most interaction with the white invaders, as Barranquito's son and successor. Although Santana was probably the most powerful of the three brothers, he kept a low profile. It is said that Cadette was a subtle and shrewd negotiator and diplomat.

Seven years after Cadette led his people out of Bosque Redondo, they reappeared when the Mescalero Reservation in the Sacramento Mountains began. This 1870s photograph of the Fort Stanton sutler's store, the original 1872 reservation rations provider, has the great sacred mountain, Sierra Blanca, in the background.

PHOTOGRAPH COURTESY OF LYNDA A. SÁNCHEZ/EVE BALL COLLECTION

John Cremony, an army captain at Bosque Redondo who wrote the first English dictionary of the Apache language and was respected by the Apaches, knew Cadette well and wrote down several of his comments during their talks at Bosque Redondo. Cremony said that, "He [Cadette] was not, so far as personal bravery goes, the leading warrior of his band, but he was the most dexterous thief." Well liked and sociable among his people, Cadette (his Apache name was Zhee-es-not-son) was said to have had seven wives and, as Cremony demonstrated from his notes, was an Apache philosopher.

Five years after Barranquito died, Cadette was peacefully camped in early November with about five hundred of his people at the water flowing out of the mouth of Dog Canyon, a major Apache access into the Sacramento Mountains, about thirteen miles southeast of present-day Alamogordo and the site of the Oliver Lee State Park. Recently appointed as commanding general of New Mexico Territory, Gen. James Henry Carlton had decided to end the Apache problem once and for all and issued orders that all Apache men were to be shot on sight even if they offered to surrender. Major William McCleave, leading two companies of Carlton's California Column, managed to surprise the Apaches at Dog Canyon and, killing many, drove the survivors to seek shelter at Fort Stanton, then under the command of Col. Kit Carson. Carson took them in and sent five Mescalero leaders with Cadette as their spokesman and their agent Lorenzo Labadie under armed guard (to protect them) to Santa Fe for a parley with Carlton, but at their meeting, there was no negotiation. Carlton said the Apaches must relocate to Bosque Redondo or face extermination and that Bosque Redondo would be their land. He already had Fort Sumner under construction for soldiers to ensure the Apaches stayed there. John Cremony recorded the answer Cadette gave to General Carlton:

You are stronger than we. We have fought you so long as we had rifles and powder; but your weapons are better than ours. Give us weapons and turn us loose, and we will fight you again; but we are worn out; we have no more heart; we have no provisions, no means to live; your troops are everywhere; our springs and waterholes are either occupied or overlooked by your young men. You have driven us from our last and best stronghold, and we have no more heart. Do with us as may seem good to you, but do not forget we are men and braves.

By March 1863, more than four hundred Mescalero men, women, and children were receiving rations at Fort Sumner and drinking bitter, alkaline water from the Río Pecos. Cremony, in many talks with Cadette, often urged him to send his children to school. Again, the Apache philosopher answered with an argument hard to rebut. Cadette said to Cremony:

You desire our children to learn from books and say, that because they have done so, they are able to build all those big houses, and sail over the sea, and talk with each other at any distance, and do many wonderful things; now, let me tell you what we think. You begin when you are little to work hard, and work until you are men in order to begin fresh work. You say that you work hard in order to learn how to work well. After you get to be men, then you say, the labor of life commences; then too, you build big houses, big ships, big towns, and everything else in proportion. Then, after you have got them all, you die and leave them behind. Now, we call that slavery. You are slaves from the time you begin to talk until you die, but we are free as the air. We never work, but the Mexicans and others work for us. Our wants are few and easily supplied. The river, the woods, and the plains yield all that we require, and we will not be slaves, nor will we send our children to your schools, where they learn to become only like yourselves.

On the night of November 3, 1865, Cadette, after telling the army many times the Apaches would not stay at Bosque Redondo, led more than five hundred Mescaleros away from the concentration camp on the Río Pecos. They went in all directions and in many different groups, making it virtually impossible for the army to follow them all and unwise to follow any. Five years later, the U.S. government was anxious to get the Apaches on a humane reservation for which Cadette said his people would return. Santana negotiated the initial framework for the reservation with the help of Dr. Joseph H. Blazer, who operated *La Maquina* (the machine), a sawmill near what is now Mescalero Village. Cadette sent word that his band wanted peace and would come in. Cadette arrived at Fort Stanton in July of 1870 and, with his usual eloquence, promised peace and even requested a school for Apache children.

Cadette settled with three of his wives near Mescalero in La Luz Canyon and attempted to farm. He kept his end of the reservation promise, but, as usual, the government did not keep its end. A few Mescaleros living near Fort Stanton scattered after hearing a rumor (believed to have been started by a whiskey bootlegger) that the cavalry planned to attack their camp. Cadette, who didn't leave, and having heard the rumor from its source, testified against the bootlegger before a grand jury in Las Cruces in early November 1872.

On November 7, 1872, Cadette left Mesilla (a village next to Las Cruces) with interpreter Juan Cojo. They were last seen on the road between Whitewater and La Luz. Chief Santana began a search for them when they failed to return. Following the trail eight miles up La Luz Canyon, he found Cadette's horse still saddled and grazing by the trail. Nearby was Cadette's corpse with a chest wound. He had ridden up La Luz Canyon until he had fallen off his horse. Cojo's sons rode in search of Cojo and found his head on a stake and bits of his clothing and blanket and his horse shot dead about twenty miles from La Luz Canyon.

According to Sherry Robinson, Eve Ball recorded two explanations for Cadette's murder. In one, the Mescaleros first believed Cojo had murdered Cadette, but then concluded that apparently both were murdered. In the second, Eve wrote that Cadette was shot during a drunken brawl by Cojo, and that Cadette lived long enough to cut off Cojo's head and set it on a pole in the road near La Luz before dropping dead after shooting his horse and staggering a short distance away. To this day, no one knows for certain what happened.

Mescaleros and White Eyes mourned the passing of Cadette. He had worked hard to keep the peace and ensure the success of the reservation. In 1873, L. Edwin Dudley, the superintendent of the reservation, blamed Cadette's murder on the Mexican bootlegger against whom he testified in Las Cruces.[1]

Natzili, Sombrero, and Solon Sombrero

NATZILI LED A VERY LARGE BAND THAT HUNTED BUFFALO AND ROAMED THE AREA around Amarillo, Texas. He was much taller than the typical Apache and powerfully built. He was the only one strong enough to draw his bow. Natzili's people depended on buffalo for food and hides for trade. The western Apaches were particularly fond of trading for buffalo hides for their tipis, since buffalo never went farther west than the Tularosa Basin in south-central New Mexico. Daklugie, youngest son of Juh and nephew of Geronimo, told Eve Ball that even the Nednhi Chiricahuas living in the Sierra Madre had buffalo-hide tipis when he was a child.

Natzili and his people, following spring and fall migrations of the buffalo, often fought with the Comanche, Kiowa, and Kiowa-Apache over the land and hunting rights. Natzili's people have a legend about a prolonged fight with the Comanche that lasted perhaps ten days, no one knows where or when, that nearly exterminated the band. After this fight, Natzili and the remnant took refuge with the Mescaleros living in the Sacramentos and settled on the slopes of the great mountain, Sierra Blanca, where their ranchería was easier to defend than in the open. Even so, the Comanche still attempted occasional raids before they were finally driven off. Natzili's people intermarried with the Mescaleros living in the mountains, and all Mescaleros acknowledged Natzili as a great chief.

In autumn, Apaches of all bands often raided deep into Mexico. During this time of year, smart, wealthy Mexican landowners left a corral filled with horses for the raiders to take, and the Apaches left the families and other property alone. If the Mexicans didn't cooperate or were too poor to freely supply them cattle or horses, the Apaches took what was there—usually women and children—the boys, if young enough, to be made into warriors, the girls to become wives of warriors, the older women to be slaves. On one of these raids, the son of Natzili encountered a wealthy Mexican wearing a sombrero glittering with four pounds of silver and mounted on a magnificent horse with a beautiful saddle, bridle, and spurs inlaid with silver. Natzili's son killed the Mexican and took the horse, saddle, and bridle, and all the other bright, shining things. He wore the wealthy man's inlaid belt and carried the sombrero, and from that day forward was known as Sombrero.

Photograph of Chief Natzili, ca. 1903. Note his plains Indian–style dress and long spear used for hunting buffalo.

PHOTO COURTESY OF NEW MEXICO STATE UNIVERSITY LIBRARY, ARCHIVES AND SPECIAL COLLECTIONS

When Sombrero's son was born at the Mescalero agency, someone familiar with the classics suggested he be christened Solon, after the great Greek philosopher, and it was so. Before Solon was five, Sombrero was fatally injured when his horse fell on him. As he lay dying in his tipi, he had his treasures brought to him. He called for Solon and, in front of witnesses, gave him the silver inlaid spurs and belt and, in doing so, pointed out that the conchos on the belt were round, as made by some Apaches, and not the usual ovals found on Mexican belts. The saddle, bridle, and sombrero were buried with Sombrero.

Before Solon had completed six years at the agency school, Natzili was taken in late 1897 or early 1898, for reasons unknown (but probably at the direction of agent Stottler), by soldiers and held for questioning in the adobe building the agency used for a jail. During a blizzard, Natzili, still very strong as an old man, managed to pull the bars off a window and escape into the storm, his tracks covered by wind and snow. Three weeks later, hunters found his body frozen near a spring on the reservation.

Natzili's grandson Solon went to school at Albuquerque and studied hard in order to return and improve the miserable living conditions of most of his people on the reservation. He converted to the Dutch Reformed Church, served as its pastor's interpreter on the reservation, and was mainly responsible for the pastor having a permanent residence on the reservation at Mescalero Village. Solon was elected to the tribal council and became its chairman (the modern equivalent of a chief). He was largely responsible for the adoption of the system used by the tribal government today. He married Chief Peso's daughter, Catarina, and together they had a great family. Just before he died at age eighty-seven, he gave the spurs and belt his father had given him to Eve Ball, the great chronicler of Apache oral history.[1]

Magoosh, Chief of the Lipan Apache

THE GREAT LIPAN APACHE CHIEF MAGOOSH WAS BORN AROUND 1830 IN MEXICO. HE is said to have remembered seeing the Alamo fall in 1836. Like nearly all Apaches, the Lipan hated the Mexicans and would have aided the men defending the Alamo if they had been able to do so. In their wild and free days, the Lipan Apaches roamed in south Texas and Mexico in the winter and moved back north toward the Sacramento Mountains during the summer. Magoosh roamed mostly from Roswell to the Guadalupe Mountains and, with Mescaleros, often attacked wagon trains headed for the California goldfields or anyone on the San Antonio–El Paso Road.[1]

Sometime in the late 1850s, the Lipan suffered an attack from a virulent form of smallpox. They were certain they had gotten it from the Mexicans, but they weren't sure how. When they killed an enemy they took only their shirt and ammunition belt, and suspected that they had gotten the disease from the shirts. Their medicine men could do nothing with the disease except watch the victims die. Magoosh called a council where it was decided that if the Lipan bands stayed together there would probably be more deaths than if they separated into smaller groups. A headman was assigned for each group, and it was agreed that, when the disease disappeared, the bands would reassemble when the chief chose a time and place.

Magoosh led his band to the Mescaleros living in the Sacramento Mountains. In 1872 Apache agent A. J. Curtis claimed he counted 350 Lipan at Mescalero, and it's likely they were under the leadership of Magoosh.

In 1876 Natzili and his band left off fighting the Comanche and trying to hunt rapidly disappearing buffalo to join his Mescalero cousins on the reservation in the Sacramento Mountains.[2] In 1877 a smallpox outbreak forced all the Mescalero bands to separate into small groups and live apart scattered over the reservation.

On April 16, 1880, the army swept down on the Mescalero Reservation to take their horses and disarm all the Apaches living there because they believed the Mescalero were supporting Victorio with warriors and weapons.[3] However, the army didn't find the Lipan Apaches. Magoosh had left for Mexico about the same time Victorio

Magoosh, ca. 1913, great, longtime leader of the Lipans at Mescalero, was an Apache rarity. He was bald.

COURTESY OF NEW MEXICO STATE UNIVERSITY LIBRARY, ARCHIVES AND SPECIAL COLLECTIONS

did in the fall of 1879 and stayed there with friends until at least the spring of 1881 after the army had been ordered off the reservation in January 1881. When Magoosh returned, he went to Chief Peso, an old friend, and asked for permission for him and his two wives and children (who he hid on the southern end of the Sacramentos) to return to the reservation, and Peso was glad to grant it. He took Magoosh to the superintendent and asked that he and his family be reenrolled. The superintendent agreed and sent scouts to bring in Magoosh's family. Magoosh and Peso served together as army scouts during the Geronimo campaigns.

When the Lipan first broke into groups to stave off smallpox, a group under the leadership of Venego went south across the Río Grande and settled in the mountains near a small Mexican village, Zaragosa, downstream from El Paso. There, the Lipan lived on relatively friendly terms with the natives. However, times became hard. There were at least two major droughts and the Mexican army began conscripting Lipan men for scouts (the Mexicans were using two Lipan scouts when they caught Victorio at Tres Castillos in 1880). The band was fast disappearing.

Antone Apache, a bachelor who lived with the Mexican Lipan, had heard rumors of Lipan living in central New Mexico near Mescalero. Without ever having been in New Mexico and without a map, he made his way north and found the Mescalero Reservation and Magoosh. He explained to Magoosh the dire circumstances under which Venego's band lived in Mexico and asked if its members could become members of the reservation. Magoosh went to James A. Carroll, one of the best superintendents the Mescalero Reservation ever had, and made the case for bringing the Mexican Lipan to Mescalero. Carroll agreed and began work to get money and approval from his superiors in Washington to bring the Mexican Lipan to Mescalero. The decision was so long coming that Carroll eventually took matters into his own hands. With the help of the Tularosa Parish priest, Father Migeon, who wrote letters to the governor of Chihuahua for approval to bring them to the United States, and after the governor (glad to see them go) offered to provide their transportation, went to retrieve the people with funds Carroll provided him. Father Migeon was able to return with thirty-seven Mexican Lipan survivors in 1905. Carroll put them under the leadership of Magoosh and, with the reservation chiefs' approvals, gave them the same rights and privileges as the reservation Apaches.

Magoosh was the last chief of the Lipan. In looks, he was a very rare, bald Apache. In his later years, he served on James A. Carroll's advisory council with Peso and his brother Sans Peur to keep the reservation running on an even keel. He was too weak to go with the posse that tracked down Kedinchin, the Mescalero who killed Don McLane in January of 1908, and sent his son, Willie Magoosh, in his place.[4] The actual date of Magoosh's passing is about 1915, not 1900, as often cited.[5]

San Juan

SAN JUAN WAS BORN IN THE EARLY 1800S. HIS BAND, THOUGHT TO BE *NIT'AHÉNDÉ* OR *Tsehitchéndé* Mescalero Apaches, ranged along the Río Bonito and Río Hondo and in the Capitan Mountains of New Mexico. He had alliances with other Mescalero bands, Lipan Apaches, and some Comanche bands.

It is claimed that San Juan probably led the Mescaleros in the battle of Round Mountain on April 17, 1868. Round Mountain stands alone on the side of the Río Tularosa about ten miles up the canyon from the village of Tularosa. Depending on which side you ask, the one-day fight sounds like a comedy of errors, although it certainly didn't seem so at the time. Twenty-six men from Tularosa village rushed to save a Fort Stanton supply wagon that was attacked by a war party of Apaches after the wagon's military escort thought it was close enough to Tularosa to be safe and had left to return to Fort Stanton. After the attack began, the driver took cover in an old abandoned fort about a mile west of Round Mountain and sent a rider to Tularosa for help. The men from Tularosa brought their horses inside the fort and made them lie down, and then they tied them down to keep them out of harm's way. The Apaches aimed their arrows high so they fell inside the fort's walls and killed every horse. As the day wore on, the men inside the fort began to need water. During a lull in the fighting, a sixteen-year-old boy managed to crawl down to the Río Tularosa a few yards away to refill canteens. The Apaches didn't see him come from the old fort, but they did see him scrambling back and thought he was an advance guard of reinforcements. Apparently deciding any additional fighters would be too many to deal with, the Apaches took off. That night the village of Tularosa celebrated a great victory over the Apaches.

San Juan joined forces with Santana, Cadette, and Roman, all sons of Barranquito, when the Mescalero Reservation was in the early stages of formation around 1871. At that time, although the Anglos viewed politically astute Cadette as the primary chief of the Mescaleros, his brother Santana, who initiated negotiations for the reservation, was a more powerful chief, principally of the northern Mescaleros, and Roman (also known as Ramón Grande) was a minor chief of Sierra Blanca Mescaleros. Cadette was murdered in

Photograph of San Juan ca. 1883. Note his plains Indian–style dress and buffalo hunter spear.
PHOTO COURTESY OF NATIONAL ARCHIVES

1872 in La Luz Canyon after testifying in a trial against Mexicans selling whiskey to the Indians. Santana died from pneumonia in the winter of 1876 after insisting on walking back to his tipi after Dr. Joseph Blazer had taken him into his home and spent two or three weeks saving him from smallpox. With Cadette and Santana gone, San Juan and Natzili took over leadership of the Mescaleros on the reservation.

In early September of 1879, Victorio left the Mescalero Reservation and started a war that was to last a little more than a year and stretched over Arizona, New Mexico, Chihuahua, and Sonora. In March of 1880, San Juan left to bring back Caballero, who had left with Mescaleros to join Victorio. The story is unclear, but apparently Caballero decided to leave Victorio, and his warriors planned to leave with him. Victorio killed him for trying to leave and challenged any other Mescalero who wanted to leave. None did. San Juan decided to stay with Victorio.

Victorio was killed at Tres Castillos in Chihuahua in October 1880.

San Juan eventually returned to the reservation and again assumed his leadership role. He passed away in 1887. He had three sons with his wife Nagoo-nah-go. Two of his sons became chiefs: Peso and Sans Peur (Without Fear), and the third, a highly respected warrior, Crook Neck. Peso, who died in 1929, was the last Mescalero chief. James A. Carroll, highly respected Mescalero agent from about 1902 to 1912, had Peso, Sans Peur, and Magoosh for his council of chiefs to help serve and represent the people living on the reservation in the early part of the twentieth century.[1]

Peso, Last Mescalero Chief

PESO, SON OF CHIEF SAN JUAN AND HIS WIFE NAGOO-NAH-GO, WAS BORN AROUND 1850 in the Guadalupe Mountains on the Texas–New Mexico border about a hundred miles east of El Paso.[1] He was twelve or thirteen when General Carlton forced his people to live at Fort Sumner and the Bosque Redondo concentration camp in 1863. Prior to Bosque Redondo, his people roamed around Fort Stanton. They used to camp there, have horse races on the flat, and take target practice with the soldiers.

After San Juan and his family escaped Bosque Redondo, Peso occasionally joined Magoosh and his Lipan Apaches where they roamed around San Antonio, which was then just a "little town with white buildings," and farther south to the Gulf of Mexico and on into Mexico. Most of the time the Lipans of Chief Magoosh moved toward Mexico City.

Peso was given his name because he had taken much money in silver. Apparently he never used it because, according to his daughter, May Peso Second, he dug a trench and buried it. He was an expert tracker and served as an army scout during the Geronimo wars. Peso became a chief when he was twenty-eight. About that time, his band left the reservation because of the Lincoln County War and the now-famous confrontations and murders involving Billy the Kid and the Tunstall-McSween faction on one side and Dolan-Murphy on the other.

Billy the Kid and his regulators and other cowboys often stole Mescalero horses on the reservation. The Mescaleros were not allowed to defend themselves against the horse thieves until a tribal police force was first organized by agent W. H. H. Llewellyn under the direction of Thomas Branigan in 1881. A few years later, Peso was recognized in the late 1880s as a respected tribal police captain.

Peso had four children: May Peso Second, Katherine Sombrero (Solon Sombrero's wife), Alton, and Bill. Additionally, he raised a nephew, Big Mouth, a well-known Mescalero personality and the last surviving army scout (he lived to be about 103 and died in 1958).

In the early 1900s, Peso, his brother Sans Peur, and Magoosh were the council of primary leaders to advise reservation agent James A. Carroll. Magoosh represented the

Dana B. Chase photograph of Peso, ca. 1886

PHOTOGRAPH COURTESY OF LYNDA A. SÁNCHEZ/EVE BALL COLLECTION

Elk Springs area; Sans Peur represented Tule Canyon; and Peso, who occasionally lived in Tule Canyon, represented the Rinconada and the Three Rivers country. Peso and Sans Peur were part of the Mescalero Police posse that in 1908 tracked down and killed Kedinchin, the last Mescalero to kill a White Eye.

Magoosh passed away in 1915, leaving Peso as the principal chief of the Mescaleros. In 1918 a business committee was organized to manage the affairs of the tribe. Since that time the committee has been the governing body of the Mescaleros and its president, the closest thing to a principal chief. Peso passed away in 1929 and was the last principal chief of the Mescaleros.[2]

Chiricahua Prisoners of War Return
to Mescalero, New Mexico

THE MESCALERO RESERVATION DECLINED IN POPULATION MAINLY FROM ANGLO diseases such as tuberculosis, pneumonia, smallpox, and measles. With constant pressure being applied by bureaucrats in Washington to take away or reduce the size of the reservation because there were too few people living on it, wise agents advised, and Mescalero chiefs understood, the need to welcome other First Nations people to live on their reservation.

Geronimo died at Fort Sill in February of 1909. Just before his passing, Asa Daklugie, his nephew, at his own expense visited Washington to argue that the Chiricahuas be released to the Mescalero Reservation. Daklugie went to the reservation to determine if the Mescaleros would accept Chiricahua and Mimbreño prisoners of war released from Fort Sill captivity and if the reservation was a good place to live. He went during hunting season when "venison was at its best" and rode over the reservation with several Mescaleros that he knew. He looked forward to and enjoyed the hunting, but with Carlisle School training in cattle management and being in charge of the Fort Sill Chiricahua herd, he wanted to check out the reservation's resources and capabilities. What he saw made him "very happy." It would support many more people than were living there without depleting its resources, and it would support cattle ranching, which the Chiricahuas wanted to do. He asked the Mescaleros, "Do you want us?" The Mescalero chiefs, Sans Peur, Peso, and Magoosh, answered, "Come to us."

Daklugie returned to Fort Sill and told the Apaches what he had seen and of the Mescalero offer to share their reservation. The prisoner of war elders formally sent an independent committee to New Mexico to see and confirm what Daklugie had told them and to check the possibility of the Mimbreños returning to their old reservation at Ojo Caliente. The committee of five formal representatives consisted of Eugene Chihuahua (son of the great leader Chihuahua) and Goody representing the Chiricahua, Kaywaykla and Toclanny representing the Mimbreños, and an army officer. Eugene Chihuahua said he rode over the reservation and found it better than Daklugie had described it. It was

Mescalero agency looking southeast in 1906 as it probably appeared to Chiricahuas arriving from Fort Sill, Oklahoma, in 1913

PHOTO COURTESY OF NEW MEXICO STATE UNIVERSITY LIBRARY, ARCHIVES AND SPECIAL COLLECTIONS

much like their homeland had been on Turkey Creek. Then the Mimbreño representatives visited Ojo Caliente and found only a few sections were available to returning prisoners of war. White settlers, after John Clum had moved the Mimbreños to San Carlos, had bought most of the good land, and heavy rains had eroded what was left.

On August 22, 1909, the prisoners of war met with First Lt. George Purington at Cache Creek on the Fort Sill Military Reservation to express their desires for a place to live when they were released. There were 259 persons (eighty men, sixty-four women, twenty boys and fourteen girls age twelve or older, and forty boys and forty-one girls younger than age twelve). Thirty-eight heads of households wanted to go to Mescalero, eighteen wanted to go to Ojo Caliente, and fourteen wanted to remain at Fort Sill. Lieutenant Purington recommended that all their cattle be sold to avoid spreading tick-borne "Texas Fever" and that the herd could be successfully disposed of for the greatest benefit to the Apaches by December 1911.

After much paperwork and bureaucratic maneuvering, the freed prisoners of war who wanted to go to Mescalero arrived by train at the Tularosa station with their possessions on April 4, 1913. They were met at the station by the new Mescalero agent C. R. Jefferis,

Ted Sutherland, superintendent of livestock, and a few tribal police to help with the move. Jefferis had been chief clerk under former agent James A. Carroll and also followed Carroll's wise practices. The Chiricahuas had brought their wagons, household goods, farming tools, and horses, but they had been strictly forbidden to bring cattle or dogs. However, according to Sutherland, when the doors were opened, "dogs simply boiled out of the freight cars."

After riding over the reservation, the Chiricahuas, all except the outcast, Chato, chose to make their homes at White Tail, about twenty-three miles from Mescalero and about eight thousand feet above sea level. Chato chose to live at Apache Summit, about ten miles east of Mescalero, where he had to haul water. The Chiricahuas and Mescaleros regarded Chato as a traitor because he had been an army scout and a San Carlos spy for Lt. Britton Davis. Davis called Chato the finest man, red or white, he had ever known.

After being moved to Fort Sill, the Chiricahuas had found living in houses convenient, and while they lived in tents for a while at Mescalero, after four years of wrangling with the Department of Interior, they were able to secure houses. The Mescaleros, who had fought being forced to live in cabins by Lieutenant Stottler in 1898 and had "reverted" to living in tipis, decided that they, too, wanted houses after the Chiricahuas got theirs.

After being moved three times as prisoners of war, the Chiricahuas never moved again after they were freed. They had been in captivity for twenty-seven years before their move to Mescalero.[1]

Naiche, Last Chief of the Chiricahua Apaches

THE CHIRICAHUA APACHES WERE RELEASED AS PRISONERS OF WAR AFTER TWENTY-seven years of captivity and most moved from Fort Sill, Oklahoma, to the Mescalero Reservation in 1913. The last chief of the Chiricahua was the second son of Cochise, Naiche, who died at Mescalero in 1919, six years after the move from Fort Sill.[1]

Naiche, youngest son of Cochise and his principal wife Dos-teh-she, daughter of Mangas Coloradas, was born around 1856. Naiche saw a ten-year war against the Americans begin when he was five years old in 1861 and end in December 1872 when Cochise agreed to live on a reservation managed by Cochise's friend Tom Jeffords. The reservation included the Chiricahua and Dragoon Mountains and Sulfur Springs Valley in between. On his deathbed in 1874, Cochise made Taza and Naiche swear to keep peace with the Americans.

Two years later, a factional fight broke out between the Chiricahuas accepting Taza as chief and one of Cochise's best warriors, Skinya, his brother, Poinsenay, and twelve followers who disputed Taza being chief and wanted to break out of the reservation. The Indian Office used this as pretext to move the Chiricahuas to San Carlos and sent John Clum to move them.

In a fight between the two factions on June 4, 1876, Naiche shot and killed Skinya and Taza wounded Poinsenay, and six of the others were killed. John Clum arrived the same day, and after talks with Naiche and Taza, convinced them to leave the Chiricahua reservation and move their people to the one Clum managed at San Carlos. In early September of that year, Taza went on a well-received tour of the East with John Clum and twenty other Apaches. However, during a stop in Washington he caught pneumonia and unexpectedly died.

Naiche was many things—a warrior, a good-looking ladies' man, a dancer, drinker, and feast lover—but, at nineteen, he was not ready to assume the chieftainship thrust on him after Taza died. Even more important to the Chiricahuas was that he had no Power—no supernatural gift that would reveal enemy plans or location, deflect bullets, or cure illness. Geronimo became his *di-yen* (medicine man) and advisor, but despite appearances, they were not close friends.

1898 F. A. Rinehart photograph of Naiche in his army uniform
PHOTO COURTESY OF LIBRARY OF CONGRESS

Naiche, remembering the American military betrayals of his father, followed Geronimo's lead in reservation breakouts, costing many lives on both sides. The deathbed promise to Cochise to keep peace with the Americans guided Naiche until 1881 when, fearing for the safety of his people, he led them off the reservation in 1881 and 1885 in large measure because he didn't trust army motives. In the ten years prior to 1886, when Geronimo surrendered, Naiche had spent six and a half years on the San Carlos and Turkey Creek Reservations. By contrast, Geronimo was on the reservation about five years, and Nana and Mangas about four years. Mangas and Geronimo led the final breakout in 1885. Naiche and Chihuahua followed, fearful of army retaliation, after Geronimo lied and told them that Lt. Britton Davis and Chato had been assassinated when they definitely had not. Only 34 men and 110 women and children left the reservation in the last breakout, and of the 80 Chiricahua men left on the reservation, 58 (73 percent) answered General Crook's call to serve as scouts during the hostilities that lasted for fifteen months.

Initially after the 1885 breakout, Chihuahua, Geronimo, Naiche, and Mangas operated independently. However, Naiche and Chihuahua soon joined with Geronimo leaving only the small group led by Mangas operating quietly in Mexico. The Geronimo group surrendered to General Crook on March 27, 1886. That night, with whiskey supplied by a bootlegger named Tribolett, the Apaches went on a major drunk. The next morning it was reported that Naiche was lying on the ground unable to stand and the others weren't much better off. General Crook went on to Fort Bowie to report the news and terms of the surrender to General Sheridan (Commanding General of the Army), leaving Lt. Marion Maus and his scouts to escort them on to Fort Bowie. Still suffering hangovers, the Apaches made little progress that day and had another drinking spree at their next camp.

Early the next morning, Naiche's second wife, E-clah-heh, tried to run to Lieutenant Maus's camp with news that Geronimo and Naiche's families planned to escape. Naiche shot her in the leg to stop her, but she made it to Maus's camp. She went on with Maus and the other surrendering Apaches and recovered from her wound. Convinced by Tribolett that Geronimo would be hanged when they crossed the border, the families of Geronimo and Naiche and a few other warriors broke away from the march north and continued the fight until they surrendered on September 4, 1886, after General Miles promised a new and better reservation and no more than two years exile in Florida, both of which were lies. The leaders were immediately sent to Fort Bowie, and while waiting for the slower members of their little band, they bought new clothes and boots with money they had taken from Mexicans on their raids in Mexico. When the others arrived, they all were sent to Bowie Station by wagon for the train taking them to Florida.

In Florida the warriors were left at Fort Pickens on Santa Rosa Island in Pensacola Bay and their families were taken on to Fort Marion at St. Augustine. The warriors at Fort Pickens were reunited with their families eight months later in April of 1887 when the army, moving the St. Augustine Apaches to Mount Vernon Barracks, let the women and children of the Fort Pickens prisoners off the train to rejoin their men. Naiche was reunited with his three wives, Nah-de-yole (the oldest), E-clah-heh, and Ha-o-zinne (the youngest and the one appearing with him in pictures taken in 1884). One observer of the Apaches at Fort Pickens described Naiche as, "... a very manly fellow and [he] exercises a good influence on the others." In 1888 the Naiche and the Geronimo group at Fort Pickens were moved to the Mount Vernon Barracks to live with the rest of the Chiricahuas.

In 1891 Naiche and forty-five others at Mount Vernon were allowed to join the army (they were still prisoners of war), and thirty-one from Apache bands at San Carlos also enlisted and were brought from Arizona to form Company I of the Twelfth Infantry. They lived under the same conditions as other enlisted men, received the same pay, and were under the same regulations. They wore army uniforms, had their hair cut, and received given names by which they were known thereafter. They conducted fieldwork with bridge building, scouting, trailing, and skirmishing and spent much time building houses on a new village site at Mount Vernon. By 1894 their terms of enlistment were up, and the War Department determined that they would be free to return to Arizona, but their families were still held in captivity. Naiche and all but two unattached young men chose to stay with their prisoner families.

In October 1894 Naiche and the other prisoners were moved to Fort Sill, where they learned the techniques of the range cattle industry, built homes, and raised crops. Captain Hugh Scott (later to become Major General Scott, Chief of Staff of the Army and Ad-Interim Secretary of War), who was initially in charge of the Apaches at Fort Sill and helped begin and manage their cattle herd, wrote, "[Naiche is] a straightforward, reliable person. When he was in charge of the cattle herd, I could depend on him completely in every weather, and he never disappointed me." Additionally, Naiche was often sent to the same expositions and parades as the much more famous Geronimo and was a widely respected figure and representative of his people.

All the old warriors passed away in captivity. Geronimo, the most famous, died near the end of February 1909, and his death was the trigger for the government bureaucracy to decide the prisoners of war should be freed. Those who wanted to return to New Mexico and the Mescalero Reservation could do so. Of the prisoners of war, 183 decided to move to Mescalero. In April 1913, Naiche, his wife Ha-o-zinne, five of his children, his mother, Dos-teh-she, two half sisters, and Ha-o-zinne's parents and half brother all moved to Mescalero. Naiche left behind in the Fort Sill cemetery his first two wives and eight of his children. Within a year after the move to Mescalero, Naiche's wife and his mother had passed away. After six years on the reservation, Naiche, who died in 1919, had his regrets. Eve Ball wrote, "He was a handsome man in his youth and a tragic figure in his age. He felt that he had failed his people and grieved over it 'til he died." Today, Naiche is an admired man of history.

The Parallel Lives of Mangas, Son of
Mangas Coloradas, and Naiche, Son of Cochise

MANGAS WAS BORN ABOUT 1840. HE MARRIED DILTH-CLAY-IH, DAUGHTER OF VICTO-rio. Later in his life, Mangas married, but in Florida divorced, Huera, a Mimbreño woman, who, along with four other Apache women, was captured and taken as a slave after the Mexican army wiped out Victorio. After four years of captivity, these women escaped a hacienda outside Mexico City and with only a knife and a blanket walked more than twelve hundred miles in six months across Chihuahua and New Mexico to return to Fort Apache and their families. Huera had learned to be a skilled maker of *tiswin*, a mild corn beer that Mangas loved to drink.

By the time he was twenty, Mangas would see three brothers die in battles, one led by Cochise and two led by Victorio. Mangas was about twenty-two when U.S. Army soldiers under Col. Joseph Rodman West murdered his father. Thereafter, he followed the lead of Victorio until Victorio was killed at Tres Castillos in October 1880.

By comparison, Naiche, youngest son of Cochise, was born in 1856. He saw a ten-year war against the White Eyes begin when he was five years old in 1861. In that year, Lieutenant Bascom hanged close relatives of Cochise after he disavowed any responsibility for the kidnapping of Felix Ward (also known as Mickey Free). Cochise groomed Naiche's older brother, Taza, to become chief of the Chokonen band of Chiricahuas. On his death-bed in 1874, Cochise made Taza and Naiche swear to keep peace with the Americans. Two years later in 1876 Taza went to Washington with John Clum, caught pneumonia, and unexpectedly died.

Naiche assumed the chieftainship after Taza died, but having no personal gifts of Power he depended on Geronimo as his *di-yen* (medicine man) and advisor. Naiche had three wives, but Ha-o-zinne, the last one surviving in 1913 when the Chiricahuas returned to Mescalero, died of a heart attack soon thereafter.

Remembering the American military betrayals of their fathers drove Mangas and Naiche to make decisions at critical points that led to reservation breakouts that cost many lives on both sides. Each man had a peaceful nature and, if they had been treated

1884 Frank Randall photographs of Mangas and Naiche (right), last surviving sons of the great Apache chiefs Mangas Coloradas and Cochise

PHOTOS COURTESY OF LIBRARY OF CONGRESS

fairly, would have been content to live on reservations. Naiche left in 1881 and 1885 and Mangas in 1877, 1879, and 1885 in large measure because they didn't trust army motives. Mangas, who not only didn't trust the army but also hated the "forty acres of hell" (as Lt. Britton Davis called the San Carlos Reservation) on which he was forced to live, longed to return to his ancestral lands around Warm Springs in the Black Range of New Mexico.

The deathbed promise to Cochise to keep peace with the Americans guided Naiche until 1881, when, fearing for the safety of his people, he left the reservation with Geronimo, but he returned from the Sierra Madre with General Crook's expedition in 1883. Mangas and Geronimo led the final breakout in 1885. Only 34 men and 110 women and children left the reservation in the last breakout.

After the initial breakout in 1885, the bands operated individually for a while under Chihuahua, Geronimo, Naiche, and Mangas. In a short time, the bands under Naiche and Chihuahua united with Geronimo's with no apparent hard feeling about his lies that had driven them from the reservation in the first place. However, Mangas and his little band never united with the others.

Mangas and band of eleven (three men and eight women and children) lived off the land in Mexico until he decided to try to slip back to his ancestral homeland in the New Mexico Black Range. He got as far as Fort Apache, where he learned from an Apache cook serving a cavalry unit that Geronimo had surrendered over a month earlier and that his band had virtually no chance of making it to the Black Range without engaging in a fight with army troopers. He surrendered to the army near Fort Apache, Arizona, on October 18, 1886. Mangas was the last Apache leader in the 1885 breakout to surrender.

Mangas died a prisoner of war at Fort Sill, Oklahoma, in 1901. He was about sixty years old. Naiche died on the Mescalero Reservation in 1919 after leaving prisoner of war captivity at Fort Sill in 1913. He was sixty-five years old.[1]

Asa Daklugie: "It Took Four Years to Get Him to Talk"[1]

DAKLUGIE WAS THE YOUNGEST SON OF JUH, THE GREAT NEDNHI APACHE CHIEF. IN October 1883, Juh's horse tumbled off a bank and into Río Aros in Chihuahua, Mexico. Juh died in the arms of twelve-year-old Daklugie, who held his father's head out of the water while his brother Delzhinne rode for help. Juh never regained consciousness and was buried on the Aros by the warriors who had come to help save him. Juh and Geronimo were brothers-in-law, and with the passing of Juh, Geronimo took over Juh's men. Daklugie and his brothers rode with them.

When Geronimo surrendered in September of 1886, fifteen-year-old Daklugie was then riding with Mangas, who surrendered in October 1886, six weeks after Geronimo, and became a prisoner of war with the Chiricahuas and Mimbreños. Daklugie, along with his future wife, Ramona Chihuahua, and a number of other Apache children and teenagers were sent to Carlisle Indian School at Carlisle Barracks, Pennsylvania. The girls were segregated from the boys, and the next day, as Daklugie told Eve Ball, "The torture began. The first thing they did was cut our hair . . . without it, how would *Ussen* recognize me in the Happy Place? . . . the bath wasn't bad . . . we liked it . . . but our breechcloths were taken, and we were ordered to put on trousers . . . We'd lost our hair, and we'd lost our clothes; with these two we'd lost our identity as Indians . . . they marched us into a room and our interpreter ordered us to line up with our backs to the wall. I went to the head of the line because that's where a chief belongs. Then a man went down it. Starting with me he said, 'Asa, Benjamin, Charles, Daniel, Eli, Frank.' Frank was Mangas's son. So he became Frank Mangas and I became Asa Daklugie . . . Our interpreter [who was Betzinez] told me it was wise to do everything required, like it or not, and to do it cheerfully. Nobody who had been a warrior for three years needed to be reminded of that. We'd been trained more rigidly before we came there than we were at Carlisle . . . Before the winter was over, I was learning to read. My teacher was a white lady, and she was very patient and kind to us. She taught us to write, too, and she was not as bossy as most

Asa Daklugie in 1910 at Fort Sill, where he was responsible for managing the Apache cattle herd
PHOTO COURTESY OF LYNDA A. SÁNCHEZ/EVE BALL COLLECTION

white ladies are. She was polite. She seemed to know without being told that I wanted desperately to be able to read, and she helped me . . ."

Daklugie was at Carlisle Indian School for about eight years. In the summers, he worked with Dutch farmers in the area and, determined that the government would not make the Apaches into farmers, learned everything he could about cattle. Raising cattle was the nearest thing to hunting and fishing that he knew and less degrading to a warrior than anything else the Americans did to make a living. He returned to his people at Fort Sill in 1895 and saw that the Apache cattle herd was in bad shape. After a scuffle over a misunderstanding of his intentions, Capt. Hugh Scott, the commander of the post, put Daklugie in charge of the herd. By the time the Fort Sill Apaches left for Mescalero in 1913, the Apache herd was one of the best in Oklahoma.

Ramona and Daklugie married in 1896. Ramona had become a Christian, but Daklugie continued to hold his Apache spiritual beliefs. They married in the Apache way with Ramona in a beautiful buckskin gown, and then in a Christian ceremony, she wore a beautiful silk dress. Their marriage was to last fifty-plus years.

In October 1905, Stephen Melvil Barrett began transcribing the memoirs of Geronimo with Daklugie acting as his interpreter. Geronimo refused to let them take transcription notes as he spoke, leaving Barrett to write from memory what he had been told.

In 1909 Geronimo died and, after twenty-seven years, the government ended the Apache prisoner of war internment four years later. Some Chiricahuas chose to leave Fort Sill, others stayed. Daklugie and a number of the Fort Sill Apaches moved to the Mescalero Reservation in New Mexico in 1913 and there began permanent homes and a new cattle herd.

The Last White Eye

THE LAST WHITE EYE killing by a Mescalero Apache occurred on the Mescalero Reservation on January 12, 1908. The killer, Kedinchin, was a former *di-yen* (medicine man) who at the time had one eye and was stone-deaf.[1]

Kedinchin (also known as Eye Covered) was a powerful medicine man on the Mescalero reservation. In 1889 he tried to heal a nineteen-year-old boy who had been attacked with two witch's weapons and was wasting away. Kedinchin's Power allowed him to remove one of the weapons (a short sliver of human bone carved to look like an arrow, painted red on the point and nock and blue on the shaft and wrapped with four human hairs) from the boy. This was after Kedinchin was warned by his Power that he would lose an eye if he did so. Kedinchin told his Power he wanted to heal the boy and didn't care if he lost an eye. After removing the first weapon, he tried to remove the second weapon two days later, but the witch's Power was stronger than his, and he failed. Four days after removing the first weapon, Kedinchin's right eyeball burst. The boy he was trying to heal continued to waste away and eventually died. By 1908, all we know of Kedinchin is that he was totally deaf, was working on a Mescalero road maintenance crew, and had a wife named Minnie.

For years ranchers ran cattle on the excellent high Mescalero pastures without paying the Mescaleros anything. The Mescalero agents finally imposed a fee of a dollar per head per year for cattle and twenty-five cents per head per year for sheep for grazing rights. The ranchers often ignored the fees, but the Mescaleros played their game by taking a few cattle for food while the ranchers looked the other way. As long as they weren't caught in the act of stealing or butchering beef, nothing was said, and no one dared ride up on someone butchering beef in an isolated spot on the reservation.

Roy McLane, foreman at the Flying H ranch, paid his grazing fees and was on good terms with the Apaches. One evening on the way home, he discovered a gate had been left open and a few cows had wandered off onto the reservation. The next day he sent his brother, Don McLane, a young rodeo rider from Oklahoma who knew little or nothing about ranching or the unwritten New Mexico range codes about stealing or butchering

Probable photograph of Kedinchin, ca. 1890
PHOTO COURTESY OF NEW MEXICO STATE UNIVERSITY LIBRARY, ARCHIVES AND SPECIAL COLLECTIONS

cattle. Roy tried to explain the local customs about Apaches and butchering range cattle to the young man, but he didn't listen.

Don McLane didn't return with the cattle the day he went after them. The next day, Roy followed his brother's shod horse's easy-to-follow trail to the reservation. At Mescalero, he learned Don had stopped at the trading post and was seen going over a ridge by Paul Blazer at the sawmill. Roy searched until dark without success. The next day he hired a couple of Apache trackers to help him, and they found and followed the trail up into the mountains where they found Don McLane's horse still saddled with its reins entangled in the brush, and nearby, Don's frozen corpse and a partially butchered beef. Don had been shot through the head. The experienced foreman didn't take long to figure out that his brother had surprised a man who knew the penalty and was butchering stolen beef.

Roy and the trackers carried the frozen body down to the agency. James A. Carroll, who had been at the agency for six years, suspected the boy had surprised the butcher and caused the killing. Carroll knew if he let outside law officers come on the reservation there would be serious trouble and decided to let the tribal police handle it, and Roy McLane agreed.

It was soon determined that the only Mescaleros missing from the reservation were Kedinchin and Minnie. It all made perfect sense. The boy had surprised deaf and half-blind Kedinchin at his butchering. Don must have ridden right up to the Apache before he knew the boy was there, and in reflexive surprise, Kedinchin killed him. Now Kedinchin and Minnie were on the run through the mountains in the dead of winter. Twenty tribal policemen and Roy McLane picked up the trail at Minnie's tipi and followed the trail south. When it led off the reservation, a county sheriff's posse joined them. They followed the trail south for four days, the Apaches sleeping outdoors under blankets and pine straw, the posse going to ranches for the night, and Roy McLane supplying food.

Suddenly, the Apaches couldn't seem to find the trail anymore. McLane and the posse, thinking they had given up, left for Alamogordo. Early the next morning, the tribal police found and killed Kedinchin somewhere in Grapevine Canyon, carrying out justice in their own way without White Eye interference. After carrying the body to Alamogordo to show the sheriff and prove that he had been taken, they carried Kedinchin back to Mescalero, where he was given a warrior's burial.

Epilogue

Since 1887, Apaches have fought government attempts to end their tribal culture through various congressional laws. The 1887 Dawes Act has been used, among other things, to break up tribes as social units, reduce the costs of reservation administration, sell off large parts of tribal lands, and make the land the tribes retain worthless by requiring generation to generation division of land among successive heirs until hundreds, even thousands of people might have ownership claims to an acre of reservation land. In 1887 reservations covered 138 million acres. By 1934, when Congress passed the Indian Reorganization Act, reservation land had been reduced by two-thirds to 48 million acres and the remainder sold to Anglos. Subsequent court cases have restored some land taken through the Dawes and Indian Restoration Acts and in some cases required payment for mineral rights for land not returned.

In the 1920s the Mescaleros fought off repeated attempts by New Mexico Senator Albert Fall, later to be Secretary of Interior under President Warren Harding, to turn their reservation lands into a national park and to take water rights they claimed as theirs for private use. In the 1950s the Mescaleros successfully defeated attempts through the Indian Reorganization Act to terminate their tribe, and in 1978 were granted full legal rights to practive native religion, which can include the use of peyote as a hallucinogen.

First Nations People were granted full U.S. citizenship in 1924, this after many First Nations young men had fought bravely and heroically in WWI and were granted citizenship in 1919. Apache scouts played a significant role helping General Pershing in the U.S.'s Punitive Expedition against Pancho Villa in Mexico in 1916/1917. The scout Tzoe was to become General Pershing's personal scout during the expedition. The young Mescalero boy, later to be known as Charlie Smith, who was taken by Geronimo's warriors at the same time they took Ih-tedda, who became Geronimo's wife and mother to Lenna and Robert Geronimo, was also a scout in the Punitive Expedition against Pancho Villa and served with Gen. Omar Bradley. Charlie later became chief of the Mescalero police and was a judge on the tribal court.

After their release from prisoner of war captivity, two-thirds of the Chiricahuas at Fort Sill chose to move to Mescalero in 1913 and selected the White Tail area on the reservation as their place to live. They had to live in tents they brought with them for four years until agent C. R. Jefferis, frustrated with long bureaucrat delays in obtaining funds, built them the houses they requested using funds from the sale of reservation timber. The Chiricahuas asked Jefferis to use the money from the sale of their outstanding cattle herd at Fort Sill to buy more cattle for beginning their new herd at White Tail. Asa Daklugie, who was in charge of the herd at Fort Sill, managed the herd at Mescalero and served on numerous tribal councils. Lenna and Robert, daughter and son of Ih-tedda, who Geronimo divorced and sent back to Mescalero in 1889 because he feared for her life as a blue-coat prisoner, were the only two of Geronimo's children to survive long enough to carry on his family. Lenna died young but had children. Robert passed away at Mescalero in 1966, leaving four children and their families. Viola Massai, one of the daughters Massai had to leave when he jumped from the prisoner of war train heading east to Florida, went to the Carlisle Indian Industrial School and was good friends with Ramona Chihuahua, Eugene Chihuahua's sister. Chief Chihuahua insisted Eugene marry Viola when Eugene had wanted to marry other girls. Eugene told Eve Ball that he and Viola loved each other, but were not in love. Viola and Eugene had six children, but they all died young. After they left Fort Sill and settled at Mescalero in 1913, Viola was able to locate her family members on the reservation, including her brother and sisters by Massai's second wife. Eugene married twice after Viola passed away. His third wife was Jennie Peña, and it was a long and happy marriage.

After Stottler left, the Mescaleros returned to living in tipis, using their cabins as storage houses. When the Chiricahuas got their houses, which were a significant improvement over the log cabins Stottler had directed to be built, the Mescaleros began to have greater interest in living in houses and life in the tipis slowly disappeared. Some continued to live in tipis, at least in the summer, into the 1950s.

Massai was killed in 1911, but his sometime-partner-in-crime, Apache Kid, lived up to his name and came to a mysterious end. There were many claims by different individuals and posses in the following years that they had killed Kid, but proof that would allow payment of the big reward was never forthcoming.

Fort Pickens in Pensacola and Fort Marion in St. Augustine, Florida, Mount Vernon Barracks just north of Mobile, Alabama, and Fort Sill, Oklahoma, where the Chiricahuas were held as prisoners of war, now show their times there through historic site markers, museums, and graves. The Chiricahuas spent eighteen years at Fort Sill, and some of their families still have their homes at or near Fort Sill. The Chiricahuas who moved to Mescalero still prosper. The great old chiefs Chihuahua, Loco, Nana, and Geronimo and many Apache wives and children are buried at Fort Sill. Naiche, the last hereditary chief of the Chiricahuas, became a devout Christian, joined the Dutch Reformed Church, took the name Christian Naiche, and signed his name that way many times. He also named a son Christian.

In Arizona, in New Mexico, in the Blue Mountains and deserts of Chihuahua, and in Sonora, where the Apaches struggled to rule the land and preserve their lifeways in their epic saga of war and survival, the wind whispers in the silence. The sun casts its fiery light on rolling sands, deep canyons, shallow arroyos, rugged mountains, and dark green creosotes spread out like oceans dotted with islands of light green mesquites, and yuccas with crowns of white. Only fearless, unyielding people who took their life from the land and valued individual freedom above all else survived there. In their struggles they left many graves and much blood, their own and their enemies scattered across the land. They did not disappear when they surrendered to an innumerable enemy with unlimited resources. Even today their children still know the old lifeways and their stories still roam the places of their fathers and grandfathers speaking to us of their courage, strength, and heroism.

Endnotes

Introduction
1. The information about the regional bands comes from Peter Cozzens, *The Earth Is Weeping*.
2. Most of the cultural information comes from Morris Opler, *An Apache Life-Way*; James Haley, *Apaches: A History and Cultural Portrait*; and Eve Ball, Lynda A. Sánchez, and Nora Henn, *Indeh*.
3. See part 4, chapter 1.
4. Paul Andrew Hutton relates a striking example of Apache honor in his book *The Apache Wars* (p. 196).

Apache Warrior Women
1. Eve Ball revealed Lozen in 1970 with the publication of *In the Days of Victorio*. Eve was able to confirm Kaywaykla's account with other Apaches she interviewed for her records of their oral histories.
2. Sweeny and Utley, respected historians, have expressed disbelief in Kaywaykla's stories about a warrior woman named Lozen, and that she was just a folklore myth. However, Paul Andrew Hutton in *The Apache Wars* agrees with Eve Ball that Lozen was a true and respected warrior.
3. Sherry Robinson writing in *Apache Voices*, a book based on Eve Ball's oral interview files.

"My Father Was a Good Man; He Killed Lots of White Eyes"
1. The details of this story are told by Lynda Sánchez in "Red Hot Chili Weapon," *True West Magazine*, p. 30, March 2012.
2. Most of what we know about the life of Juh comes from Daklugie, who told his stories to Eve Ball. They are recorded in Eve's classic book with Lynda Sánchez and Nora Henn, *Indeh*. He also served as the interpreter for his uncle, Geronimo, when he told S. M. Barrett his life story in *Geronimo, His Own Story, The Autobiography of a Great Patriot Warrior*.

Juh's Assassination of Lt. Howard Cushing
1. The Apaches through the voice of Daklugie, Juh's son, claim in Eve Ball, Lynda Sánchez, and Nora Henn's book *Indeh* that it was in fact Juh who directed the killing of Lieutenant Cushing.

Victorio
1. The information for the Victorio story is drawn mainly from *In the Days of Victorio, Recollections of a Warm Springs Apache*, by Eve Ball; *Apaches: A History and Cultural Portrait*, by James L. Haley; and *Conquest of the Apachería*, by Dan Thrapp. *In the Days of Victorio* is the story of James Kaywaykla, who died in his sleep at Fort Sill, Oklahoma, June 27, 1963, a very old man, told to Eve Ball. Kaywaykla's "grandfather" (great-uncle by American reckoning) was Nana.

Geronimo and the Arroyo Fight
1. Most of the information in "Geronimo and the Arroyo Fight" comes from Angie Debo's biography, *Geronimo*, and Sherry Robinson's *Apache Voices*, which was written using the files of Apache oral histories kept by Eve Ball.

The Geronimo Wars

1. The Geronimo Wars stories draw most of their information from Angie Debo's biography, *Geronimo*; S. M. Barrett's *Geronimo, His Own Story, The Autobiography of a Great Patriot Warrior*; and Eve Ball, Lynda Sánchez, and Nora Henn's *Indeh*.

Geronimo's First Breakout from San Carlos, 1878

1. The Apaches have an entirely different version of this story, which Sherry Robinson records in her story of Eskiminzin in *Apache Voices*.

Al Sieber, Chief of Scouts

1. Information for this chapter is found in the excellent biography *Al Sieber*, by Dan Thrapp.

Apache Scout Tzoe, "Peaches"

1. See part 1, chapter 8, "Geronimo and the Arroyo Fight."

Chato: Survivor and Apache Judas?

1. Another hint at why the other scouts were accepted by the Chiricahuas comes in a note Eve Ball sent to Dan Thrapp, who wrote *The Conquest of Apachería*. Eve said, "Once pointed out to me, it seemed logical that the scouts were not so loyal as officers portrayed them. Obviously, Gatewood [who with Gordo and others talked Geronimo into his final surrender in 1886] questioned it. The old Apaches didn't [view the scouts as disloyal] for they knew that what he [Gatewood] said was true: that the scouts provided others with ammunition and at times protected their friends and relatives when the officers believed them absolutely reliable." This suggests that Chato, as a scout, was probably a lot closer to what army officers believed about the scouts than what the Chiricahuas knew they often did, and, in the end, it probably made a difference in how they treated Chato.

The Apache Kid: Trials, Escape, Renegade

1. The stories in this part are based on information in the excellent biography *The Apache Kid*, by Phyllis de la Garza.

Massai—The Warrior Who Escaped

1. The Massai stories are based on the stories Alberta Begay, youngest daughter of Massai, told Eve Ball, who with Lynda Sánchez and Nora Henn recorded them in her Apache oral history, *Indeh*.

Apache Prisoners of War at Mount Vernon Barracks

1. Eugene Chihuahua, son of Chief Chihuahua, described Apache captivity at Mount Vernon to Eve Ball, who recorded his story in her book *Indeh* with Lynda Sánchez and Nora Henn. Additional details are also provided by Ange Debo from the research provided in her biography, *Geronimo*.

Apache Prisoners of War Sent to Fort Sill

1. Information for the story of the Apache movement from Mount Vernon Barracks in Alabama to Fort Sill comes from Ange Debo's biography, *Geronimo*, and Eugene Chihuahua's story recorded by Eve Ball and told in *Indeh* with Lynda Sánchez and Nora Henn.

Apache Prisoner of War Years at Fort Sill

1. Most of the information for this story comes from Angie Debo's biography, *Geronimo*, and Apache oral history from several sources interviewed and recorded by Eve Ball with Lynda Sánchez and Nora Henn in *Indeh*.

Geronimo Asks President Theodore Roosevelt to Let His People Go

1. Quoted in Angie Debo's biography, *Geronimo*, p. 420.

Geronimo's Twenty-Three Years in Captivity

1. Most of the information presented in this story is from Ange Debo's biography, *Geronimo*, and Eve Ball, Lynda Sánchez, and Nora Henn's record of Apache oral history, *Indeh*.

2. Eugene Chihuahua, a "grandson" (Eugene's grandmother, Francesca, married Geronimo after she escaped from Mexico), and Daklugie, his nephew, told the story of his death to Eve Ball, who with Lynda Sánchez and Nora Henn recorded it in their Apache oral history book, *Indeh*. Note that this story differs from that told by Angie Debo in *Geronimo*, and others where Geronimo, after getting drunk, was riding his horse home and fell off into an irrigation ditch near his house and lay there most of the night before he was discovered and eventually taken to the Apache hospital.

The Mescaleros Penned Up at Bosque Redondo

1. This story and the next describes the events leading up to and the Apache disappearance from Bosque Redondo using information found in *The Mescalero Apaches*, by C. L. Sonnichsen, and Apache oral history preserved in *Indeh*, by Eve Ball, Lynda Sánchez, and Nora Henn.

Five Hundred Mescaleros Disappear Overnight from Bosque Redondo

1. T*he Mescalero Apaches*, by C. L. Sonnichsen, and *Indeh*, by Eve Ball, Lynda Sánchez, and Nora Henn.

Victorio on the Mescalero Reservation

1. Most of the information for this story comes from *The Mescalero Apaches*, by C. L. Sonnichsen, and *Apache Voices*, by Sherry Robinson

2. See also part 8, chapter 10, "The Last White Eye."

The Jicarilla Come to Mescalero

1. Most of the information for this story comes from *The Mescalero Apaches*, by C. L. Sonnichsen, and *The People Called Apache*, by Thomas E. Mails.

Agent V. E. Stottler, Tata Loco

1. *The Mescalero Apaches*, by Dr. C. L. Sonnichsen, and V. E. Stottler's article in *New Outlook*, Volume 56, 1897, provided most of the information used in this chapter.

"Kill the Indian . . . Save the Man"

1. Much of the information for this story comes from *The Mescalero Apaches*, by C. L. Sonnichsen, V. E. Stottler's article in *New Outlook*, and *Education for Extinction*, by David Wallace Adams.

Cadette

1. *Apache Voices*, by Sherry Robinson, and *The Mescalero Apaches*, by C. L. Sonnichsen, provided background information for this chapter.

Natzili, Sombrero, and Solon Sombrero

1. Information for this story comes from *The Mescalero Apaches*, by C. L. Sonnichsen, and *Indeh*, by Eve Ball, Lynda Sánchez, and Nora Henn.

Magoosh, Chief of the Lipan Apache

1. See part 1, chapter 2.
2. See part 8, chapter 2.
3. See part 7, chapter 4.
4. See part 8, chapter 10.
5. Most of the information in this story is from *Indeh*, by Eve Ball, Lynda Sánchez, and Nora Henn.

San Juan

1. This story sketches major events in the life of Chief San Juan with information from the Eve Ball files presented by Sherry Robinson in *Apache Voices*.

Peso, Last Mescalero Chief

1. See part 8, chapter 4.
2. Most of the information for this story is from *Apache Voices*, by Sherry Robinson, using Eve Ball's interviews with Peso's daughter May Peso Second and son Alton.

Chiricahua Prisoners of War Return to Mescalero, New Mexico

1. Much of this information comes from Eve Ball's interviews with Chiricahuas who remembered making the move, which were recorded with Lynda Sánchez and Nora Henn in the classic work *Indeh* and Angie Debo's biography, *Geronimo*.

Naiche, Last Chief of the Chiricahua Apaches

1. Most of the information in this story is from the oral histories recorded by Eve Ball and published in her book, *Indeh*, with Lynda Sánchez and Nora Henn.

The Parallel Lives of Mangas, Son of Mangas Coloradas, and Naiche, Son of Cochise

1. Edwin Sweeny, who wrote biographies of Cochise and Mangas Coloradas, describes in *From Cochise to Geronimo, The Chiricahua Apaches, 1874–1886* how the sons of Cochise and Mangas Coloradas reacted in similar ways and for similar reasons to reservation life as a result of their fathers' treatment by the American military.

Asa Daklugie: "It Took Four Years to Get Him to Talk"

1. Eve Ball, a retired schoolteacher who lived in Ruidoso, New Mexico, on the edge of the Mescalero Reservation, began recording the life stories of Apaches who walked by her door and stopped for a cool drink of water and to talk. It took her four years to get Daklugie to tell his stories, which are recorded in her book, *Indeh*. In April 1955, Daklugie brought her three boxes of his personal papers and photographs for her reference. He died a week later.

The Last White Eye

1. The sources of information on Kedinchin include *Indeh*, by Eve Ball, Lynda Sánchez, and Nora Henn, *The Mescalero Apache*, by C. L. Sonnichsen, and "Indian Justice," by Dr. Irving McNeil, in the *New Mexico Historical Review*, Vol. XIX (October 1944), pp. 261–70.

Additional Reading and Information Resources

Adams, David Wallace. *Education for Extinction.* Lawrence: University Press of Kansas, 1995.

Austerman, Wayne R. *Sharps Rifles and Spanish Mules: The San Antonio–El Paso Mail 1851–1881.* College Station: Texas A&M University Press, 1985.

Ball, Eve. *In the Days of Victorio: Recollections of a Warm Springs Apache.* Tucson: University of Arizona Press, 1970.

Ball, Eve, Lynda A. Sánchez, and Nora Henn. *Indeh: An Apache Odyssey.* Norman: University of Oklahoma Press, 1988.

Barrett, S. M. *Geronimo, His Own Story: The Autobiography of a Great Patriot Warrior.* New York: Meridian, Penguin Books USA, 1996.

Bourke, John G. *An Apache Campaign in the Sierra Madre.* Lincoln: University of Nebraska Press, 1987. Reprinted from the 1886 edition published by Charles Scribner and Sons.

———. *On the Border with Crook.* New York: Charles Scribner's Sons, 1891.

Cozzens, Peter. *The Earth Is Weeping.* New York: Alfred A. Knopf, 2016.

Cremony, John C. *Life Among the Apaches.* Lincoln: University of Nebraska Press, 1983.

de la Garza, Phyllis. *The Apache Kid.* Tucson, AZ: Westernlore Press, 1995.

Debo, Angie. *Geronimo: The Man, His Time, His Place.* Norman: University of Oklahoma Press, 1976.

Goodwin, Grenville, and Neil Goodwin. *The Apache Diaries: A Father-Son Journey.* Lincoln: University of Nebraska Press, 2000.

Goodwin, Grenville. *The Social Organization of the Western Apache.* Original Edition Copyright 1942 by the Department of Anthropology, University of Chicago; Century Collection edition by the University of Arizona Press, Tucson, AZ, 2016.

Haley, James L. *Apaches: A History and Culture Portrait.* Norman: University of Oklahoma Press, 1981.

Hutton, Paul Andrew. *The Apache Wars.* New York: Crown Publishing Group, 2016.

Mails, Thomas E. *The People Called Apache.* New York: BDD Illustrated Books, 1993.

McNeil, Dr. Irving. "Indian Justice," *New Mexico Historical Review,* Vol. XIX (October 1944), pp. 261–70.

Opler, Morris Edward. *An Apache Life-Way: The Economic, Social, and Religious Institutions of the Chiricahua Indians.* Lincoln: University of Nebraska Press, 1996.

———. *Apache Odyssey: A Journey Between Two Worlds.* Lincoln: University of Nebraska Press, 2002.

Robinson, Sherry. *Apache Voices: Their Stories of Survival as Told to Eve Ball.* Albuquerque: University of New Mexico Press, 2003.

Sonnichsen, C. L. *The Mescalero Apaches.* Norman: University of Oklahoma Press, 1973.

Stottler, V. E. "A Practical View of the Indian Question." *New Outlook,* Volume 56, The Outlook Company, First Edition, June 12, 1897.

Sweeney, Edwin. *From Cochise to Geronimo: The Chiricahua Apaches, 1874–1886.* Norman: University of Oklahoma Press, 2010.

Thrapp, Dan L. *Al Sieber: Chief of Scouts.* Norman: University of Oklahoma Press, 1964.

———. *The Conquest of Apachería.* Norman: University of Oklahoma Press, 1967.

Utley, Robert M. *Geronimo.* New Haven, CT: Yale University Press, 2012.

Worchester, Donald E. *The Apaches: Eagles of the Southwest.* Norman: University of Oklahoma Press, 1992.

INDEX

A

Advance Guard, The (painting), 17
Albert (Massai's son), 88, 90
Alchisaye, 58, 59
American Horse (Chief), 111
Antonio, 5
Apache, Antone, 153
Apache Ambush, An (painting), 74
Apache Kid. *See* Kid, Apache
Apache Lifeway, An (Opler), 102
Apache Medicine Song (Remington), 126
Apache (movie), 77
Apache Odyssey, A Journey Between Two Worlds (Opler), 102
Apache on the Trail (painting), 57
Apacheria, area of, iv, xii
    See also Apaches
Apaches
    bands of, xii–xiv
    culture of, xi–xii, 176–78
    family life of, xviii–xxi
    at Fort Sill, 103, 104–6, 107–10
    and Gen. Crook's rules, 41–42
    language of, xiv
    at Mount Vernon Barracks, 96–99
    portrayal of in popular culture, xi
    as prisoners of war, 91–92, 93–95
    raiding and warfare of, 1–2
    religious beliefs of, xvi–xviii
    as scouts, 49, 50–53, 56, 57, 58
    training and honor of, xxii–xxiii
    women warriors of, 3–4
    See also specific tribes, individuals
Apache Scouts Trailing (painting), xii
Apache Warrior (painting), 14
Arizona Territory, judicial system in, 69
Askadodilges (Hides His Foot), 102

Athabascan (language), xiv
Attach on the Stagecoach (Hansen painting), 5
Avott, Jesus, 70, 71, 72, 73, 75
Azul, 116

B

Bach-e-on-al, 71, 72, 75
Ball, Eve, xi, 53, 65, 108
    on Apache scouts, 56
    on Cadette, 146–47
    and Daklugie, 65, 170
    and Eugene Chihuahua, 177
    and Kaywaykla, 3, 4
    on Naiche, 166
    and Solon, 150
Barranquito (Chief), 144, 145, 154
Barrett, Stephen Melvil, 110, 172
Bascom, George Nicholas, 167
    and Cochise, 13, 15
Baylor, John R., 5, 6
Bedonkohes, territory of, xiii
    See also Mimbreños
Beneactiney, 60, 63
Beyer, Charles D., 18–19
Big Mouth (Scout), 53, 85, 157
Billy the Kid, 157
Bi-the-ja-be-tish-to-ce-an, 71, 72, 75
Bi-ya-neta, 100
Blazer, Dr. Joseph H., 17, 18, 127–28, 146, 156
Blazer, Paul, 174
Blue Mountain Apaches. *See* Chiricahuas
Bonito (Chief), 29, 39, 42
    raid by, 60, 63
Bosque Redondo, Mescaleros at, 119–21, 122–24, *144*, 145, 146, 157
Bourke, John, xxiii, 10, 49, 58
Bradley, Omar, 102, 176

Branigan, Thomas, 132, 133, 134, 136, 157
Buckskin Charlie (Southern Ute), 111

C
Cadette (Chief), 118, 143, 144–47, 154, 156
    at Bosque Redondo, 120, *122,* 123
Caje, 128
Carillo, José, 127
Carlisle Indian Industrial School, 96, 142
Carlton, James Henry, 119–21, 122, 123, 124, 143,
    145, 157
Carr, Eugene Asa, 37
Carroll, James A., 90, 153, 162
    council of chiefs of, 156
Carson, Kit, 120, 121, 145
Cavalryman's Breakfast on the Plains, A
    (Remington), 129
Central Chiricahuas, territory of, xiii
    See also Chiricahuas
Cha (Chief), 143
Chappo, 98–99, 142
Chase, Dana B., photo by, 158
Chato, 42, 52–53, 63–65, 162
    raid by, 60
    surrender of, 22
Cherokees, 94
Cheyenne, 2
Chihenne People. *See* Eastern Chiricahuas
Chihuahua, Eugene, 25, 55, 106, 160, 177
    at Fort Sill, 108
    and Geronimo, 113, 114–16
    at Mount Vernon Barraks, 97, 98
Chihuahua, Ramona, 106, 108, 109, 170, 172, 177
Chihuahua (Chief), 25, 91, 118, 164, 165, 169
    buried at Ft. Sill, 177
    death of, 91
    goes to Mexico, 42
    photo of, 115
    raid by, 60
    surrender of, 22
Chippewa, language of, xiv
Chiricahuas, xiii, 30, 31, 43, 65, 177
    and Asa Daklugie, 93
    family life of, xx, xxi
    in Florida, 46, 81–82, 91, 93–94, 165
    at Fort Sill, 22, 46–48, 52, 95, 103–6, 107–10,
        143
    at Mount Vernon Barracks, 96–99
    as prisoners of war, 91–92, 96
    on reservation, 91, 100, 118, 160–62, 163, 165,
        176–77

scouts, 58
    in Sierra Madres, 27, 29
    at Turkey Creek, 80
    warriors of, xii
Chokonen Chiricahuas. *See* Chiricahuas
Chokonens. *See* Central Chiricahuas
Chunz, 58
Cibecue Apaches, xiii
    See also Western Apaches
Civil War, beginning of, 5
Cleveland, Pres. Grover, 46, 93, 133
Clum, John, xi, xxiii, 111, 125, 161, 167
    and Chiricahuas, 163
    and Geronimo, 15
    photo of, 32
    and San Carlos reservation, 31–33, 34–35, 39
Clum, Woodworth, xi, 111
Cochise, xiii, 10, 167
    and Bascom, 13, 15
    battle at Apache Pass, 119
    death of, 78
    and Jeffords, 163
    and San Carlos reservation, 31
Cojo, Juan, 146–47
Comanches, xii, 2, 103, 128
    and Jicarilla, 134
Cowart, Fletcher J., 133, 136
Crawford, Capt., 43
Cremony, John C., xviii, 1, 145
    on Apache women, 4
Crook, George, xxi, xxiii, 81, 99, 165, 169
    and Apache scouts, 49, 50, 51, 52, 58
    attack in Mexico, 39, 40
    attack in Sierra Madres, 27, 29
    capture of Apaches, 23
    and Chato, 63
    and Chiricahuas' surrender, 46, 47, 48
    and Davis's telegram, 55
    and Geronimo's last breakout, 42–43
    meeting with Geronimo, 43–44
    and Nana, 22
    photo of, 41
    on resettling Apaches, 95, 103
    resignation of, 91
    rules for Apaches, 41
    and Tzoe, 60
Crook Neck, 156
Cross Eyes, Katie. *See* Ih-tedda
Cross Eyes, Robert. *See* Geronimo, Robert
Cumpah, 100
Curtis, A. J., 151

Curtis, Edward S., photos by, xviii, 89
Cushing, Lt. Howard, 10–12

D
Dah-tes-te, 3, 4
Daklegon, 7
Daklugie, Asa, 7, 56, 113, 170–72, 177
    on buffalo-hide tipis, 148
    on Carr's attack, 37, 39
    on Chato, 65
    and Chiricahuas, 118, 160
    at Fort Sill, 106, 108–9, 110
    and Geronimo's death, 116
    on Juh and Cushing, 10, 12
    and Juh's death, 8–9
    and Robert Geronimo, 102
    and Roosevelt, 111
    on Victorio's death, 16
Davis, Britton, 40, 41–42, 52, 55, 162, 169
    and Chato, 63
    on San Carlos Reservation, 125
    and Tzoe, 60, 62
Davis, Wirt, 43
Dawes Act, 47, 103, 176
Dawson, Byron, 18
Day, Matthias W., 18
Debo, Angie, 82
de la Garza, Phyllis, 75
Delshay, 58
Delzhinne, 7, 170
    and Juh's death, 8–9
Dene. *See* Athabascan (language)
Des-a-lin (Chief), xxiii
Diablo, photo of, 32
Diaz, Antonio, 68
Diaz, Porfirio, 76
di-gen (medicine man), xvii
Dilth-Clay-Ih, 167
di-yen (medicine man), xvii
Dodge, Kathrine Taylor, photo by, 82
Dos-teh-she, 163, 166
Dudley, L. Edwin, 147

E
Eastern Chiricahuas, territory of, xiii
E-clah-heh, xxi, 165
El-cahn, 71, 72, 75, 76
El Paso Road, attacks on, 5–6
Endicott, William C., 65, 68
Eskiminzim, photo of, 32

F
Fall, Sen. Albert, 176
Farny, Henry, paintings by, 2, 28, 58, 59, 74
Fatty, Eustace, 56
Fly, C. S., photos by, 24, 41, 79
Forsythe, George A., 24, 26
Fort Apache (film), 1
Fort Davis, 5, 6
Fort Marion, 96, 177
Fort Pickens, 96, 177
Fort Sill, 47, 48, 99, 103, 104–6, 107, 177
Fort Stanton, 157
Fort Sumner, 120
Fountain, Albert, 127
Free, Mickey, 13, 42
Fryer, Sheriff, 73, 75
Fun, 7, 24, 25, 26

G
García, Lorenzo, 25
Gatewood, Lt., 58
George (Apache), 39
Geronimo, xvii, xxiii, 13, 55, 60, 118
    arrest of, 15
    burial of, 177
    cattle of, 39–40
    celebrity of, 111, 114
    and Chato, 65
    and Chihuahua, 114–16
    on Davis's and Chato's death, 164–65
    death of, 91, 116, 160, 166
    final surrender of, 45–48, 52
    at Fort Sill, 104, 109, 110
    goes to Mexico, 42
    and Ih-tedda, 101–2
    and Juh's death, 170
    and Massai, 78, 79, 80
    meeting with Crook, 43–44
    at Mount Vernon Barracks, 97–98, 102
    with Naiche and Mangas, 169
    photos of, xvi, 3, 24, 38, 41, 94, 115
    raid on Fort Apache, 100
    relationship with Naiche, 163
    rescue of Mimbreños, 23, 25, 26
    return from Mexico, 39–40
    and Roosevelt, 111–13
    at San Carlos Reservation, 29, 30, 31–33, 34–36,
        37, 51–52, 164–65
    in Sierra Madres, 27, 29
    surrender of, xi, 9, 22, 29, 30, 58, 66, 67, 81, 93, 136
    on Victorio's death, 16

*Geronimo, His Own Story, The Autobiography of
a Great Patriot Warrior* (Barrett), 110
Geronimo, Lenna, 176, 177
Geronimo, Robert, 101, 102, 176, 177
Gil-lee, 42
Godfroy, Fred C., 16, 20, 126, 127
Gómez, Juan, 143
Gon-zizzie, xxii
Goodwin, Grenville, 29
Goodwin, Neil, 29
Goody (Chiricahua), 160
Goyahkla. See Geronimo
Gray Lizard, 52, 78, 79
    and Massai, 82, 83, 84

H
Hale (Apache), 72, 75
    photo of, 71
Hansen, Herman W., xii, xv, 5, 54, 57
Ha-o-zinne, xx, xxi, 165, 166, 167
Harding, Pres. Warren, 176
Harrison, Pres., 99, 103
Hart, Henry Lyman, 35
Has-kay-bay-nay-ntayl. *See* Kid, Apache
Has-ten-tu-da-jay, 71, 72, 75
Hatch, Edward, 15, 18, 130
Hoag, Ezra, 39
Hollow Horn Bear (Brulé Lakota), 111
Holmes, William, 70, 71, 72
Horn, Tom, 43, 70
Hos-cal-te, 71, 72, 75, 76
Howard, Guy, 98
Howard, Otis, 31, 98, 103
Huera, 167

I
Ih-tedda, 98, 100, 101–2, 176, 177
Indian Reorganization Act, 176
In the Days of Victorio (Ball), 3
Ishton, 7, 116

J
Jacali, 7
Jackson, William Henry, 135
Jefferis, C. R., 161, 177
Jeffords, Tom, xxiii, 15, 163
    at San Carlos reservation, 31
Jicarillas, xii, xiii, 117, 143
    boarding school for, 141
    family life of, xx, xxi

on Mescaleros Reservation, 132–33, 134, 136–37
    territory of, xiii
Juh (Chief), xiii, 7–9, 60, 116, 118
    camp of, 27
    and Cushing's death, 10–12
    death of, 8–9, 170
    rescue of Mimbreños, 23
    at San Carlos reservation, 31, 32, 36, 37, 39, 51

K
Kayitah, 52
Kaywaykla, James, 25, 26, 56, 160
    on Chato, 63, 65
    escape of, 16
    on Lozen, 3, 4
    and Nana, 21
    and Victorio, 13
Kedinchin, 118, 153, 159, 173–75
Kid, Apache, 52, 55, 66, 177
    escape of, 70–72, 73, 75–76
    and Massai, 80
    murder of "Rip," xxii, 52
    photos of, 50, 71
    trials of, 67–69
Kiowas, 2, 103
Kosterlitsky, Col., 75

L
Labadie, Lorenzo, 120, 123, 145
Ladd, Runner Ed, photo of, xx
Lancaster, Burt, 77
Le Clair, Edward, Sr., 114
Lenna, 98, 100, 101, 102
Lieber, G. Norman, 68
Life Among the Apaches (Cremony), xviii, 1
Lipans, xii, xiii, 128
    and Mescaleros, 143
    in Mexico, 151, 153
    See also Magoosh (Chief)
Little Plum (Piegan), 111
Little Star, 78
Llewellyn, W. H. H., 117, 131–33, 134, 136,
    138, 157
Loco (Chief), 22, 25, 42, 115
    buried at Fort Sill, 177
    death of, 91
    joins Geronimo, 51
    photos of, 97, 115
    rescue of, 23–24
    and San Carlos reservation, 35, 39

Lookout, The (Hansen), xv
Lorona, Andronico, 73
Lozen, 3–4, 26, 99
  and Victorio, 13

M
Magoffin, James, 6
Magoosh (Chief), 151–53, 157, 159, 160
Manchito, 128
Mangas Coloradas, xiii, 42, 78, 119
  death of, 91
  escape from train, 82
  skull of, 116
  surrender of, 9
  and Victorio, 13, 15
Mangas (son of Coloradas), 55, 164, 165, 167–69
  surrender of, 170
Martine, Charles, 52, 56
Massachusetts Indian Association, 98
Massai, 52, 75, 77, 81, 108
  death of, 88–90, 177
  early life of, 78–80
  escape of, 82–84
  wife of, 85–87
Massai, Viola, 108, 177
Mauricio, 16
Maus, Marion, 43, 44, 165
  pursuit of Geronimo, 46
McCarthy, Patrick, 6
McCleave, William, 145
McComas, Charlie, 63
McComas, H. C., 63
McIntosh, Bob, 71
McLane, Don, 118, 153, 173–75
McLane, Roy, 173, 174, 175
McLeave, William, 120
Mescaleros, xii, xiii
  belief in witchcraft, xvii
  at Bosque Redondo, 119–21, 122–24, 145,
    146, 157
  chiefs of, 143, 144
  family life of, xix, xx, xxi
  and Indian Reorganization Act, 176
  last chief of, 159
  and Natzili, 148
  near Ft. Davis, 5–6
  pastures of, 173
  reservation of, 95, 100, 117–18, 119–21, 122–24,
    129–30, 136, 146, 160
  in Sacramento Mountains, 143, *144*
  and Stottler, 138–40, 141–42

Middleton, Eugene, 70, 72, 73
Migeon, Father, 153
Miles, Nelson A., 22, 29, 30, 81, 93, 165
  and Apache Kid, 67
  and Chiricahuas' surrender, 46, 47, 48
  and Geronimo's surrender, 65
  and Lt. Scott, 103
  sends tribes to Florida, 91
Mimbreños, xiii, 13, 96
  as prisoners of war, 91–92, 93
  on San Carlos reservation, 15–16, 20, 23, 34, 35,
    38, 91, 125–26, 160, 161
  at Turkey Creek, 80
  See also Victorio
Morrow, Major, 130
Mott, Sgt. John, 11–12
Mount Vernon Barracks, 94, 96–98
Muchacho Negro, 128
My Bunkie (painting), 11

N
Nagoo-nah-go, 156, 157
Nah-deiz-az, photo of, 71
Nah-de-yole, xxi, 165
Naiche (Chief), xiii, xxi, 23, 39, 43, 46, 48, 118,
    163–66, 167–69
  after Noch-ay-del-klinne's death, 60
  conversion of, 177
  in Florida, 91
  goes to Mexico, 42
  on killings, xxiii
  photos of, xx, 3, 94, 97, 104, 115, 168
  at San Carlos reservation, 31, 51, 55
  in Sierra Madres, 27
  surrender of, 22
Nana (Chief), 13, 20–22, 37, 42, 118, 164
  buried at Ft. Sill, 177
  and Chato, 63
  death of, 91
  escape of, 130
  and Godfroy, 16
  on Mescalero Reservation, 117, 126–27
  at Mount Vernon Barracks, 97, 98
  photo of, 115
  and Victorio, 17
Nantaje (scout), 58
Natzili (Chief), 148, 149, 150, 151
Navajos, 128
  language of, xiv
  on Mescaleros reservation, 121, 122–23

Nednhis, xiii, 7
    See also Juh
Nicolás (Chief), 5–6
Noch-ay-del-klinne, 37, 60
Nolgee, 31, 32, 35
Northern Tonto Apaches, xiii
    See also Western Apaches

O
Ojo Caliente Apaches. *See* Bedonkohes
On the Border with Crook (Bourke), 10
Opler, Morris, 102
O'Sullivan, Timothy, photo by, 86

P
Parker, Quanah, 93, 111
Pash-ten-tah, 69
Peña, Jennie, 177
Perico (White Horse), 25, 100
Pershing, General, 62, 176
Peso, Alton, 157
Peso, Bill, 157
Peso (Chief), 118, 153, 156, 157–59, 160
Pierce, Capt., 67, 68
Poinsenay, 35, 163
Pratt, Richard Henry, 142
Proctor, Sec. of War, 48
Purington, George A., 116, 161

Q
Quick Killer (Tats-ah-das-ay-go), 1

R
Randall, Frank, photos by, 21, 38, 61, 64, 168
Red Clay People. *See* Eastern Chiricahua
Reed, Dr. Walter, 97, 98
Remington, Frederick, paintings by, 17, 126, 129
Reynolds, Glenn, 69, 70, 71–72
Rinehart, F. A., photographs by, xvi, 164
Rip (Apache), xxii, 67
Robinson, Sherry, 146
Roman (Chief), 143, 144, 154
Roosevelt, Theodore, 111–13
Rope, John, 26
Rowdy, 80
Running Water, 128
Russell, C. M., painting by, 14
Russell, S. A., 17–18, 20, 127, 130
Ryan, Sheriff, 73, 75

S
San Carlos Apaches, territory of, xiii
    See also Western Apaches
San Carlos Reservation, 23, 90
    Chiricahuas on, 91, 93
    Geronimo on, 27, 29, 30, 34–36, 51, 60
    Mangas on, 169
    Mimbreños on, 20, 91, 125–26, 160, 161
    Naiche on, 164
    photos of, 34, 82
San Juan (Chief), 127, 154–56, 157
Sans Peur (Chief), 153, 156, 157, 159, 160
Santana (Chief), 143, 144, 146, 154, 156
Say-es, 69, 71, 72, 75, 76
Sayler, Shorty, 73
Schreyvogel, Charles, 11
Scott, Hugh Lenox, 103, 105, 106, 107,
    166, 171
    and Daklugie, 109
    photo by, 104
Scout, The (painting), 54
scouts, Apache, 49, 50–53, 56, 57
    Chato, 63–65
    and Salt River Cave fight, 58, 59
    Tzoe, 60–62
Second, May Peso, 157
She-ga, 96, 100, 102
Sheridan, Phillip, 22, 42–43, 67, 165
    and Chiricahuas' surrender, 46, 47
Sieber, Al, xxiii, 52, 54–55, 67, 68
    and Apache Kid's escape, 67, 73
    and Reynolds, 70
    wound of, 69
Sigesh, xviii
Simms, Marion, 90
Sioux, 2
Skinya, 163
Smith, Charlie, 4, 101, 102, 176
Sombrero, 148, 150
Sombrero, Katherine, 157
Sombrero, Solon, 150
Sonnichsen, C. L., 131
Southern Chiricahuas, territory of, xiii
Southern Tonto Apaches, territory of, xiii
    See also Western Apaches
Stottler, V. E., xxi, 138–40, 141–42,
    162, 177
    and Mescalero Reservation, 117–18,
    132
Sturdevant, Eugene K., photo by, 115
Sutherland, Ted, 162

T

Tata Crooked Nose. *See* Llewellyn, W. H. H.
Taylor, Capt., 58
Taza (Chief), xiii, 163, 167
    and San Carlos reservation, 31, 32
Terrazas, Joaquín, 16, 19, 21, 130
Thrapp, Dan, 7, 19, 54
Through the Pass (Farny), 28
Tiffany, Joseph Capron, 37
Toclanny, 160
Toga-de-chuz, xxii, 67
Tonkawa, 52
Tonto Wars, 58
Tres Castillos, raid on, 13
Tribolett, 45–46, 165
Tularosa Reservation, 125
Turkey Creek Reservation, 80, 164
Tzoe, 51, 60–62, 63, 176

U

Updegraff, Capt., 123

V

Velarde, Chief James Garfield, 135, 137
Venego, 153
Victorio, Recollections of a Warm Springs Apache
    (Kaywaykla), 63
Victorio (Chief), xiii, 4, 13–16, 20, 36, 151,
    153
    ambushes by, 17–19
    death of, 167

on Mescaleros Reservation, 34, 35, 125–28
    sister of, 3
    and Terrazas, 20–21
    at Tres Castillos, 37
    wars of, 117, 129–30, 156
Victorio War. *See* Victorio (Chief)
Villa, Pancho, 176

W

Ward, Felix, 13
Warm Springs Apaches. *See* Mimbreños
Washington (Victorio's son), 37
Wayne, John, 1
West, Joseph Rodman, 167
Western Apaches, xiii–xiv
    See also Apaches
White Cloud, 78
White Eyes, 147
White Mountain Apaches, xiii, 39
    See also Apaches
Willcox, Gen., 36, 37, 39
Wratten, George, 108, 109

Y

Yahe-chul. *See* Fun

Z

Zan-a-go-li-che, 85, 86, 87, 88, 90
Zhee-es-not-son. *See* Cadette (Chief)
Zi-yeh, 98

About the Author

W. **Michael Farmer** combines ten-plus years of research into nineteenth-century Apache history and culture with Southwest-living experience to fill his stories with a genuine sense of time and place. A retired Ph.D. physicist, his scientific research has included measurement of atmospheric aerosols with laser-based instruments, and he has published a two-volume reference book on atmospheric effects on remote sensing. He has also written short stories for anthologies and award-winning essays. His first novel, *Hombrecito's War*, won a Western Writers of America Spur Finalist Award for Best First Novel in 2006 and was a New Mexico Book Award Finalist for Historical Fiction in 2007. His other novels include: *Hombrecito's Search*; *Tiger, Tiger, Burning Bright: The Betrayals of Pancho Villa*; and *Conspiracy: The Trial of Oliver Lee and James Gililland*. His *Killer of Witches, The Life and Times of Yellow Boy, Mescalero Apache, Book 1* won a Will Rogers Medallion Award and was a New Mexico–Arizona Book Awards Finalist in 2016. *Mariana's Knight: The Revenge of Henry Fountain*, *Legends of the Desert, Book 1* and *Blood of the Devil: The Life and Times of Yellow Boy, Mescalero Apache, Book 2,* published in May and June 2017 respectively, were finalists for the 2017 New Mexico–Arizona Book Awards.